Rejected

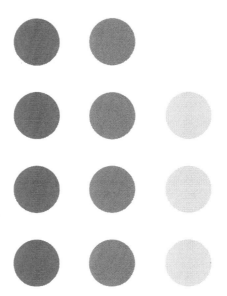

essays on belonging

Michelle Fiordaliso

HENRY GRAY
HG
PUBLISHING

Granada Hills, CA
"Select books for selective readers"

For information, contact: henrygraypub2022@gmail.com

Publisher's Cataloguing-in-Publication Data

Names: Fiordaliso, Michelle, 1972-.
Title: Rejected: essays on belonging / Michelle Fiordaliso.
Description: Granada Hills, CA : Henry Gray Publishing, 2024. | Includes 18 b&w photos.
Identifiers: LCCN 2024903283 | ISBN 9781960415189 (hardback) | ISBN 9781960415172 (pbk.) | ISBN 9781960415196 (ebook)
Subjects: LCSH: Self-realization. | Self-actualization (Psychology) in women. | Loss (Psychology). | Belonging (Social psychology). | California. | New York. | LCGFT: Essays. | BISAC: BIOGRAPHY & AUTOBIOGRAPHY / Memoirs. | BIOGRAPHY & AUTHOBIOGRAPHY / Women. | LITERARY COLLECTIONS / Women Authors.
Classification: LCC PS3606.157 2024 | DDC 814 F56—dc23
LC record available at https://lccn.loc.gov/2024903283

Made in the United States of America.

Published by Henry Gray Publishing, P.O. Box 33832, Granada Hills, California 91394

For more information or to join our mailing list, visit HenryGrayPublishing.com

Rejected
essays on belonging

Michelle Fiordaliso

with Photographs by Lindsay Morris

For anyone who has suffered rejection
or who craves a sense of belonging.

Table of Contents

Introduction

The essays in this book have all been rejected, some of them multiple times. Over the years, I've seen my work published in some of my favorite publications, including some of the most reputable. But the essays herein were either passed on or ghosted completely. As my fellow writer friend Tara says, "No answer is still an answer."

The essay is one of my favorite mediums. Essays can be short. They're often timely. And for me, they demand to be written. An unwritten essay nags at me like a toddler until I sit down and pay attention. It keeps me up at night until I turn the light on and grab a notebook or go to my desk. Sometimes an essay comes out in one complete piece, like the shed skin of a snake; other times, it takes years to craft.

No one tells you when you first start wanting to write that becoming a writer entails distinct phases. The first is believing you have things to say. The next is granting yourself permission to put those things down on paper. The third is writing and rewriting and rewriting again until the things on the page are close enough to the things you see in your head. And then, there is the part that really sucks—maybe not if you're Joyce Carol Oates or Roxane Gay, but for most of us—the part where you must convince editors that your piece belongs in their publication.

Weathering frequent rejection is integral to being an artist. There will be so many *we're-gonna-pass-on-this-one's* that you won't be able to count them. I think the film *Whiplash* isn't so much a story about an abusive teacher as it is an allegory. The industry beats you down, and you have a few choices: change careers, kill yourself (quickly,

1

with a gun; slowly, with some addictive substance), or rise to the occasion, albeit with bloody fingers.

In 12-step programs, they say *rejection is redirection.* Enough friends and colleagues have asked me, over the years, to read and reread and pass around these essays for me to decide to collect them in one place. In some way, they are all about belonging. Belonging to one's home or country. Belonging to oneself. And now I've created a place for them to belong. They were rejected and therefore redirected into this book you hold. I trust it's where these words were always meant to be.

Scout

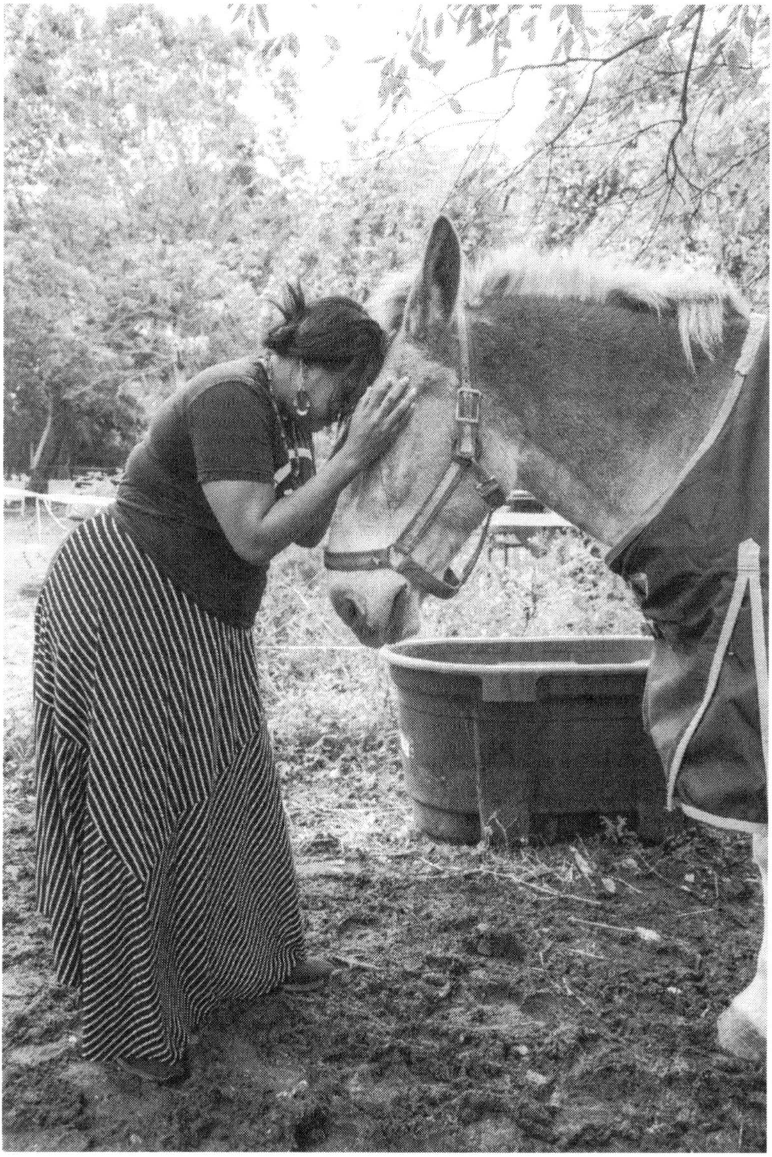

I never understood the whole *girls and horses* thing. I didn't have a horse-themed tenth birthday party. I didn't take riding lessons. I never saw *Black Beauty*. Given my background, I wouldn't have expected to learn about romantic love from a horse.

Years ago, I was asked by a friend to attend a Human-Equine retreat. Equine-assisted psychotherapy programs have been shown to be effective in treating everything from autism to eating disorders. It was going to be a weekend of communing with, interacting with, and learning life lessons from horses. As a responsible single parent, I had long ago said goodbye to the skydiving and motorcycling adventures that came before the birth of my son, but this was one adventure I could safely undertake. And the operative word for me wasn't so much "horse" as it was "retreat." Quiet time on a farm sounded delightful.

Horses weren't completely new to me. The summer prior, I had spent a weekend with the friends who would later invite me to the retreat. They had moved to the suburbs and bought a horse named Scout, and I helped them groom him. I also got to recline on the grass reading *Middlesex*. And I watched them practice cantering and galloping.

Though I knew their horse was going to be at the workshop, I wondered if I would recognize him among the herd. But when I walked down the hill, I couldn't mistake him. It was like recognizing my own child among a group. The horse is a gigantic Clydesdale with amber eyes.

As I approached Scout's pen, another workshop attendee was already standing there. I wanted to give them their space, so I walked quietly along the side of the corral toward one of the other horses, but Scout was quick to follow. He caught up with me like a dog greeting his owner. Ebullient and excited, he put his lips against my face. Playfully, he removed the name tag from my shirt with his nose. Tears flooded my eyes. How could I doubt whether I mattered to friends and family, when this creature I'd spent two days with remembered me so fondly?

The idea that I was forgettable didn't materialize out of nowhere. My son's father had had an affair with someone at work when our baby was two months old. After that, feeling secure with romantic partners didn't come easily to me. I didn't have a track record of picking safe people, so it's no wonder that I didn't feel safe. I chose people who, for one reason or another, weren't sure about me. And then I made their ambivalence a reason to feel unsure about myself.

When the leaders asked us which horse we wanted to work with one-on-one, my answer was clear: Scout. I would set my intentions with a counselor, and then spend twenty minutes in a round pen with him. The counselor and the rest of my group would observe and comment.
As a perpetual caretaker, my intention was to learn how to receive. I was tired of feeling like I was only worthy of love based on things I did or gave, rather than on who I am. As I thought about this, I noticed that Scout walked towards me. I entered the pen. For our previous interaction, we had been on opposite sides of a fence. This time, I was alone with a horse that was seventeen hands tall and two thousand pounds. The reality was that he could charge me, kick me or buck me. But would he? Was this a lesson in trust?

I didn't approach Scout right away. I waited for him to come to me, something I don't usually do with people.

And he did come towards me. Slow. Gentle. He took his time. We breathed together. I waited until I felt safe and comfortable before I reached out to touch him. I reached out to pet his nose, and he let me. He even let me hug him. He didn't move once. He didn't startle me in any way. He was constant—and in the face of that, I decompressed. So much of the anxiety I walk around with each day vanished.

When it was time to go home, I went to say good-bye to Scout, who was chewing on hay. Upon seeing me, he left the food behind, and approached. He planted what felt like a kiss on my face. I thought about relationships I'd had. It's so easy to keep working away at our desk or keep washing the dishes or talking on the phone when our partner walks in after work. Scout showed me how different it feels when someone stops what they're doing and takes the time to greet you. What if we got up from our desks and met our lovers at the door, the way dogs do? What if we took them in our arms and kissed them? *I'm so happy you're home. I've got a bit of work to do, but I can't wait to have dinner with you in an hour.*

I left the weekend knowing something I hadn't realized before. What I was looking for was not a particular person, not a particular set of physical characteristics or personal traits. What I was looking for was a specific feeling. It was a feeling of calm and love in the presence of someone else. I had gotten glimpses of it in my life. There was the married man I'd met on a summer vacation in Sicily. We sat next to each other on the beach for a month and watched our kids play in the sea. Something happened to me when I was with him. I felt safe. I wondered if it was because he was the only one with an umbrella that never blew away, or because he always had cold water and gum. Or if some alchemical connection was at play. Neither one of us crossed any boundaries, but meeting him changed me. I would never have swiped right on him on a dating app, but being around him gave me the feeling I'd like to feel from a husband someday. That feeling of safety allowed me to be my truest self. It helped me find both laughter and serenity.

Since I was a kid, I've carried a list of traits I want my person to have—things like intellect and humor, wit and worldliness. But I've been in a relationship with someone who possessed those qualities and still felt agitated in his presence. I can ascribe that agitation to the fact that he would forget to lock the door before coming to bed. Or to the fact that he'd lose his wallet all the time. I could say it was because life scared him more than it scares me. But it wasn't really any of those things—it was the lack of a certain feeling.

For me, love is about being seen, remembered, and recognized. It's about receiving. It's about being with someone big-hearted, who uses their size to protect rather than to intimidate. Scout gave me a reference point for what love should feel like. I trust that, now that I've felt it, I'll be able to recognize it when it comes.

Shouts & Murmurs

Modern-day Reasons for Rising Divorce Rates

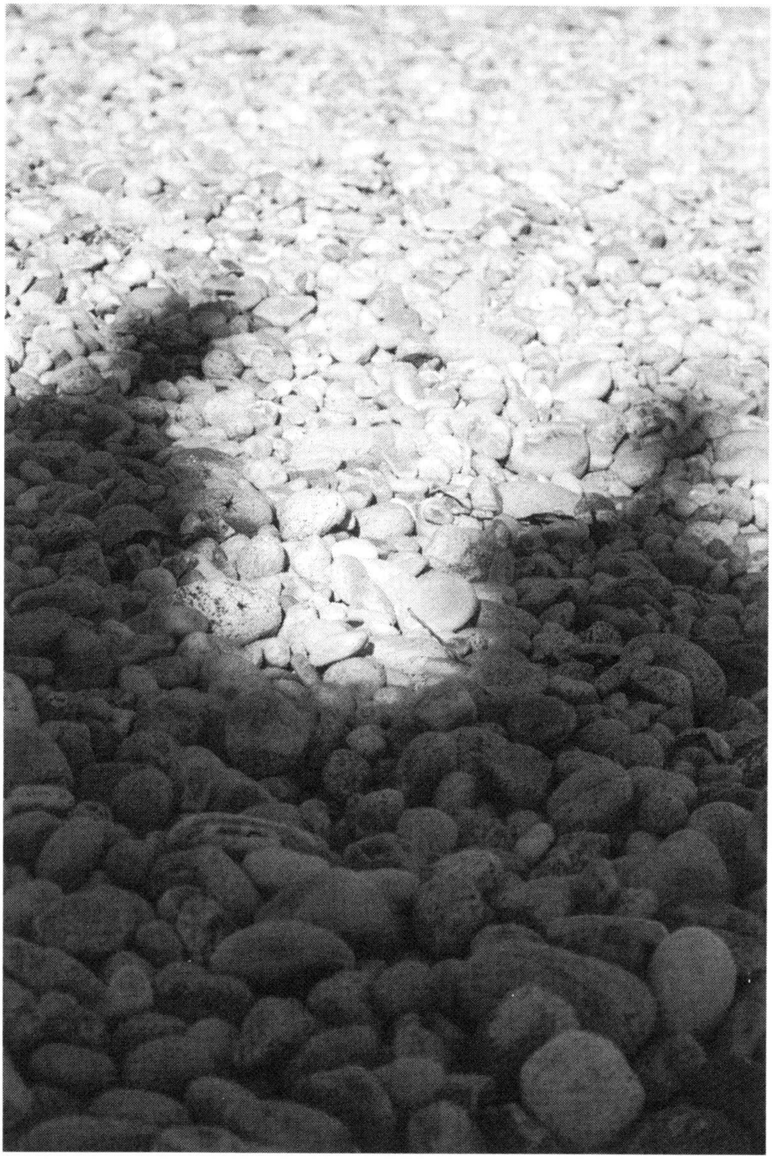

As a relationship therapist, I'm accustomed to hearing arguments about the usual things—sex, money, in-laws, having too many books. But in recent years, there's been a significant and confounding shift: an irreconcilable difference between the person someone fell in love with and the way that person represents themselves online is being cited as a leading cause of divorce.

Common conflicts among twenty-first century couples (as told to me, their shrink):

Gian loves her actual husband, Jude. It's his online persona that repulses her. "Who is this man and what the heck do his Tweets mean? He and his hashtags can go to hell."

Raul claims his wife Linda's overuse of the wink emoji is a form of flirtation. He's baffled that she doesn't see it as cheating. "I see her finger moving towards the semicolon and I start to sweat."

Jamal says his effervescent influencer-fiancé is a total drag to live with. "She's clinically depressed. How does she have her million followers convinced that she's happy?"

Despite Priya's husband Dan's constant use of LOL, he never does laugh out loud. "I don't believe him when he says he's laughing on the inside."

Manny's wife Christiane's poetry Substack is followed mostly by Mormons. Manny suspects that Christiane has a second husband in Utah. "That would explain all the calls to Salt Lake City on her cell phone bill."

Hans claims the celebrity articles his wife Layla posts on her story make her seem shallow and dumb. "A forty-five-year-old woman shouldn't care that JLo and Ben are getting married. What happened to the Ivy-League-educated doctor I married, the Habitat for Humanity volunteer?"

Tatiana doesn't like the fact that everyone can see her boyfriend Geoff's likes on conservatives' TikTok pages. "I've learned to overlook his right-wing ways—but gosh, I don't want my friends to know I'm dating a Republican."

Jill feels smothered by her boyfriend Taye's compulsion to "like" or comment on every one of her Facebook posts. "For once, I want to update my status without him noticing. Doesn't he have anything better to do?"

Carla is suspicious of her husband Eli's artful Instagram photos. "He must be gay. Not since Herb Ritts has there been a man with an eye like that!"

Erich feels his husband Hassan doesn't have enough social media followers. "I just always pictured myself with someone that had at least ten thousand followers and a verified account."

Many of my client couples did a better job connecting when conversations were whispered into one another's ears, rather than posted onto one another's walls. A genuine, audible laugh beats an LOL any day. The remedy: try taking your sweetheart on a Saturday afternoon stroll in the park, where tweets still come from actual birds.

Migration

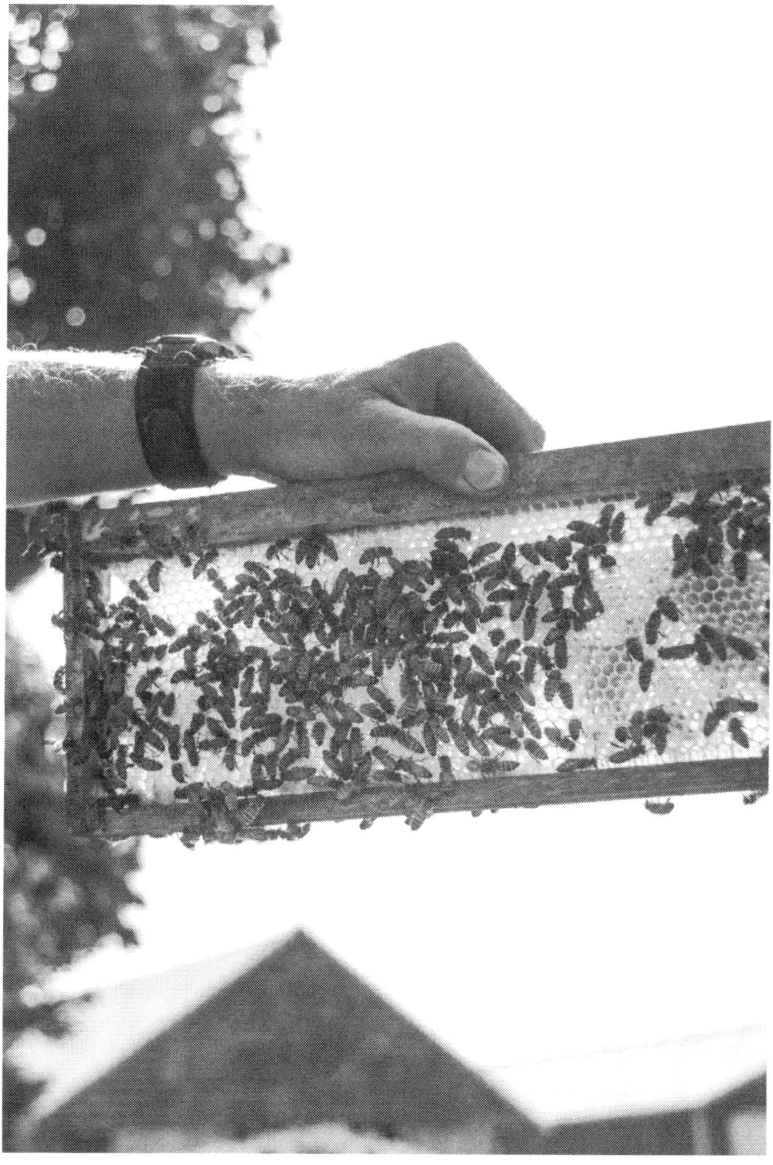

"I'm tired of the long, cold winters." That might've been a logical explanation for deciding to pick up our whole life and move from Brooklyn to Los Angeles in 2005. It had, in fact, been a frigid year—but that explanation would've been a lie. The truth was that I had never loved a place more than I loved Brooklyn. Park Slope had brownstone-lined streets, mysterious green parrots in the winter trees, and great restaurants—all without the relentless, frenetic buzz of Manhattan. I felt more at home there than anywhere.

I didn't really want to go, but somehow the borough was forcing me out. I lost my job. My landlord sold the building, and the new owner wanted to live in our apartment. That's what you get when you gut and renovate the kitchen of a rental. The lease was up on my car, and my five year-old son was about to start kindergarten. All signs seemed to point towards a new beginning.

I had often thought a job or lover would propel me to live in another place. Being a native New Yorker, I delighted in the idea of being pushed to experience another location, but that wasn't happening. As each layer of our life got stripped away that year, I thought the solution might be to rescue myself and relocate. If I took the leap, perhaps the romance and career I longed for would appear. The notion of leaving everything I knew terrified me, but I also worried that, if I stayed, I'd become complacent and never find the courage to leave.

The tipping point came when my playwriting teacher suggested I had a chance of making it as a writer in Hollywood. This was my dream, so, buoyed by hope, I scheduled our move for late August. As I planned the overwhelming logistical details, I remained naïve to how hard the task ahead of me would be: Herculean for anyone, but virtually impossible for the single mother of a child not yet in elementary school.

Friends and family didn't believe I could do it. They predicted I wouldn't last six months, but I proceeded. One day, while picking up packing tape, I walked past a store window where a bee amulet caught my eye. I thought the charm would be the perfect reminder to be industrious, to keep moving until we got to the other side. Somehow I knew that staying in a constant state of motion would protect me from getting paralyzed by fear. If I wanted to make it, I couldn't afford to let terror take over—I had to be like a bee. Bees accomplish the impossible—their bodies, too big for their wingspans, shouldn't be aerodynamic— yet the rapid speed of their wings enables them to fly. I bought the necklace, put it on, and pressed forward.

Still, even after I'd packed up half my apartment, I hoped that the man I was casually dating that summer would offer something big enough to keep me in New York so I wouldn't have to go through with my ridiculous plan. After I bought the necklace, he stopped by for a visit after a trip to Arizona and noticed the bee.

"In the Southwest, I learned something interesting about bees."

"What?" I asked.

"They migrate from one side of the country to the other."

I had known that birds and butterflies migrate, but not bees.

"In huge swarms," he continued. "Sometimes, when they hit the desert, they don't make it, and you can find tens of thousands of bees lying there dead on the sand."

This left me feeling discouraged. Was this story a cautionary tale about moving cross-country? I'd heard stories of crime in LA. Was I putting my son in peril? I only knew a few people and wondered if we'd make friends or find community. Whom would I call for soup if Joe or I got sick? I felt reckless, not having a job or much money saved or a school picked out. Was I being as foolish as other people in my life believed? Could I pull it off? Endless questions. Zero answers.

August came quickly. Joe and I arrived in Los Angeles. The city felt vast, and I didn't know where to begin. Using a small fold-out map and a borrowed car, I dragged my son from one overpriced dump to the next. Joe was hot and had stomach aches. After the first few days, I could feel my confidence wilting. There were none of the things I'd come to love about New York apartments—hardwood floors, crown moldings, a sense of personal history.

I missed the corner where I'd gotten kissed. The playground where Joe loved to slide. The block where my best friend and I sang Don Henley's "Boys of Summer" wearing vintage Levi's jeans and white Hanes t-shirts.

By the end of five days in Los Angeles, we'd seen fifty-five places. I was lonely. Joe was exasperated. Friends thought we wouldn't last more than six months; I was starting to wonder if we'd last six days.

In my notebook, I penned a list of non-negotiables for a living space. If I didn't find a place that met our needs within the next twenty-four hours, I decided, we'd return to New York, defeated and willing to eat crow. I scribbled down things like natural light, a good school district, and outdoor space. I also included a few wishes that weren't quite requirements: a fruit tree in the yard, cafés and shops within walking distance, space for friends to stay when they'd visit.

The place didn't show up. Still, I found myself driving on the 405 to sign a lease on a house I didn't like. That's when I felt an anxiety attack coming on and pulled off the freeway. With my passenger seat empty and no one to consult about this huge decision, it was as if my body were sending up flares saying I was making the wrong choice. So I regained composure, turned around, and headed in the opposite direction. Soon I was driving down a street in the city's best school district, flanked on either side by amazing Ficus trees. Then, suddenly, a For Rent sign caught my eye, and I stopped in front of a charming group of bungalow apartments.

Behind a white picket fence was a big yard with an orange tree and another tree that would be great for climbing. I called the number on the sign from my cell phone. The voice on the other end told me the door was unlocked. Once inside, I found everything on my list, both the non-negotiables and the wishes. I went to the manager's office and wrote a check.

On the evening we moved in, Joe and I approached the front door. It was dark out, but the light over the entrance to our apartment was bright. I pulled out my new set of keys and was stopped by a soft but insistent buzzing sound. The entire three-by-seven foot screen was covered with bees. Not one inch of wire mesh showed. I had never seen anything like it.

That night we used the back door. The bees were still there in the morning when I took Joe to his first day of school; by the time I picked him up and brought him home, they had gone.

Perhaps this swarm of bees had made it in their migration from one coast to the other just as we had. While I longed for someone to be there to tell me I had worked hard and done well, the bees that covered our entry reminded me we weren't alone. We had all made the long, hard journey together and we were all safe at home.

We lived in that apartment for thirteen years, from two days before Joe started kindergarten until two months after he graduated high school.

In that time, there would be many confirmations that we'd chosen the right place. The bees were just the beginning.

On Profile

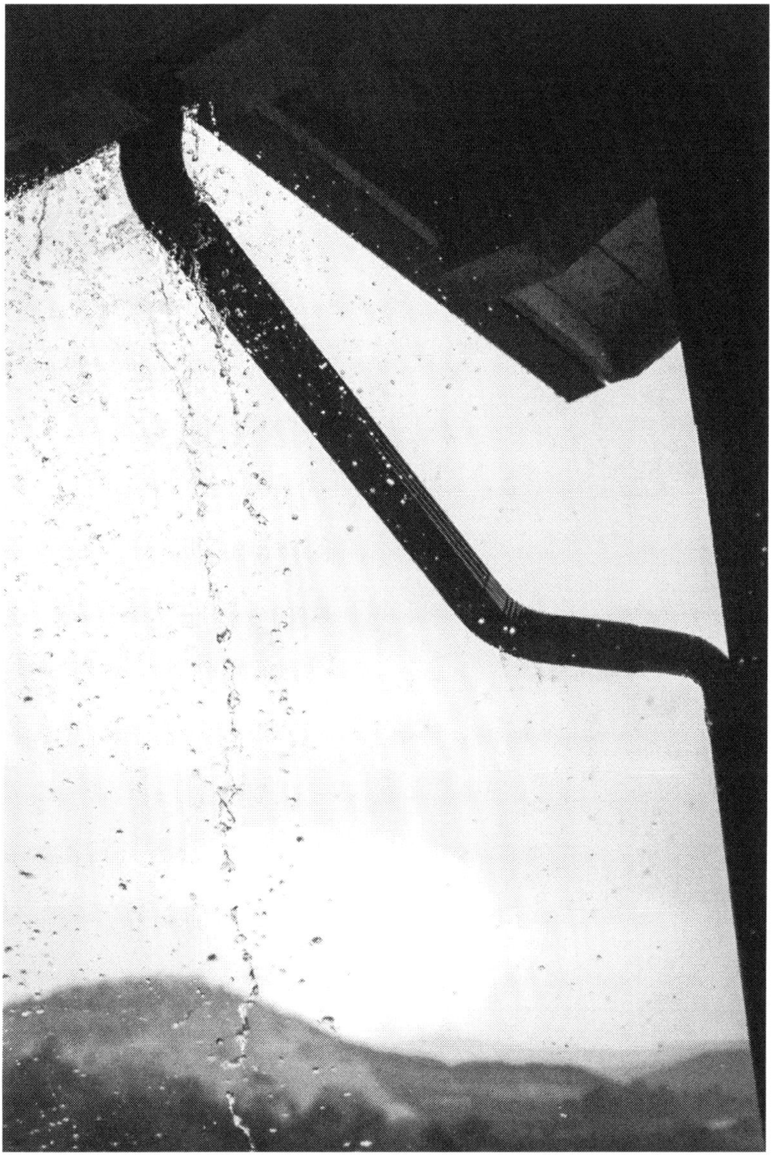

The skin on the underside of his bicep was soft and fleshy like a frog's leg or a clam. There was something I liked about grabbing it while he drove shirtless across the great plains. Iowa and Kansas. I like people's profiles better than I like a full frontal view of their faces, and sitting in the passenger seat afforded me miles and miles to study the contours of his nose, the pucker of his lips, the furrow of his brow. I enjoyed wondering what random or calculated thought might have been making him frown or smirk or even laugh for a second. I like a profile because it's less *look at me* and more *see how I see.*

On the day we drove up to Horse Tooth, we parked the car and hiked our way through Ponderosa Pines, stopping to smell the butterscotch of their bark. He was the one who taught me that their wood coating was candy-scented. Growing up in Queens, New York, I had never known anything like the Rockies. Even the foothills were bigger than any mountain I'd seen.

As we reached the top, the sky started to crack. We could see lightning in the distance. Somewhere it was pouring, and soon it would be storming. Watching the clouds move towards us across the wide, expansive vista was like looking at a weather map.

I didn't grow up knowing how to take cues from nature. I didn't know about shifts in the wind and what they meant. But I was learning. This mountain man was showing me. He was my portal into the natural world. He gave me a reason to leave a glinting silver skyline behind. The city was loosening its grip on me; something unexpected was taking hold.

"What will happen after you go back to New York?" he asked.

I thought about my East Village life. The woman I loved was in that city, our city, sleeping in our bed. The sticky humid air that forced us to walk Avenue A at night to escape the sweltering heat of a tenement apartment. The heat that made it too hot to make love—so hot that we'd have to spritz our naked bodies with rubbing alcohol and wait for the fan to oscillate our way. The 24-hour pizzeria sold a soft-serve pistachio cone for a dollar. Men and women filled Tompkins Square Park, stripped down and showing off their tattoos of swallows and saints.

"I don't know," I replied, knowing she was waiting for me to come home to her.

As the storm came closer, we sought shelter under a tree. We sat on a slab of rose quartz, our silhouette facing the streaming clouds. The sky sang us a lullaby. We listened and let the clouds soak us through.

Daily Bread

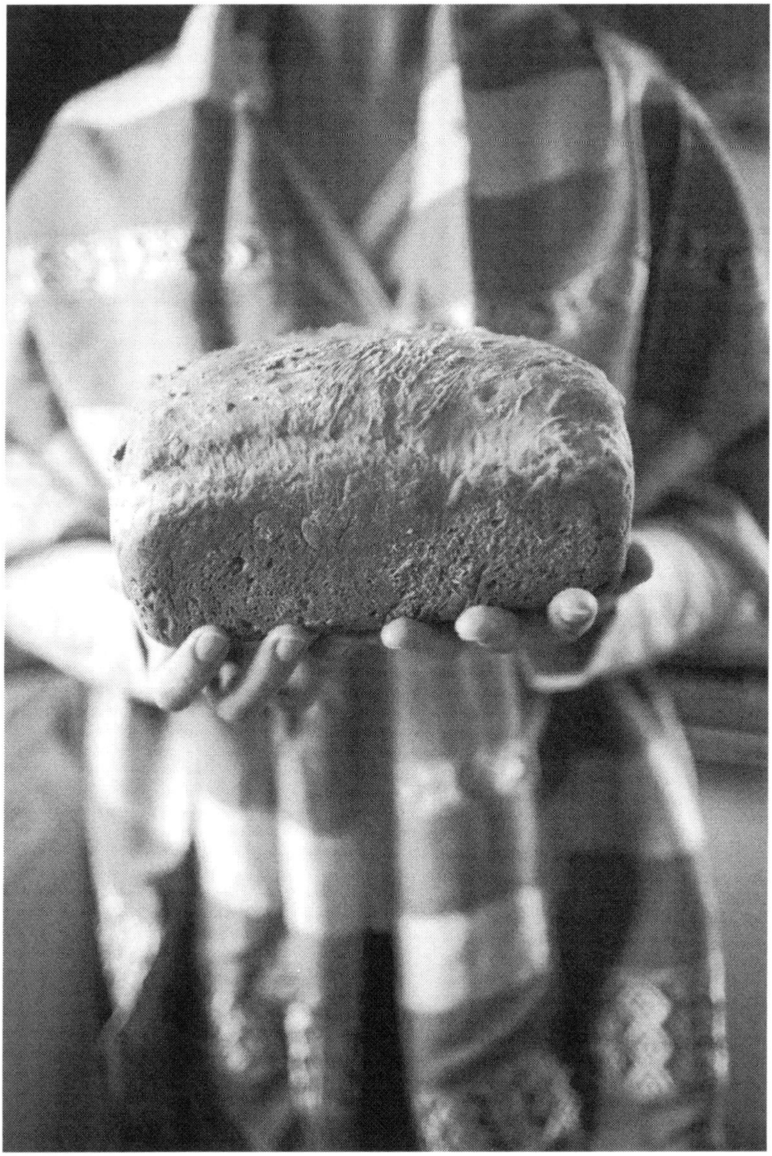

It is Paris. 2004. I walk with Laurel and Ilan. It's what we do well. We walk. We approach a small bakery. The smell of bread. A regular outing to pick up a simple staple for the house. A very young woman with strawberry-blond hair greets us. Ilan asks after her father.

Laurel and Ilan are good at making small talk with shopkeepers, befriending strangers. I am, too. We share this in common. It's the reason we're friends. Years ago, we met on the island of Jamaica, escaping the East Coast winter, seeking sun and juicy mangos and time to read on the beach. Now, years later, we walk through Paris. We each have sons, but standing in front of us is somebody's daughter.

She says her parents have died in a helicopter crash. She has left college to take over the family business— the world-famous Pain Poilâne. The city's inhabitants have eaten this bread for three generations. Sometimes smeared with butter, other times soaked in broth. The girl who stands before us asks if we'd like to see the oven.

We follow her down narrow steps into a basement with one small oven that's cooked countless loaves of bread. It has fed people after funerals, through two world wars, and on boozy, romantic nights. As I look into the tiny illuminated space, I well up with tears. The flood of feelings surprises me. I find a sense of belonging.

Apollonia's parents have died in an accident. Ilan's father was murdered years ago. In ways like these, people are taken from us. And sometimes the people we wish for don't come, and we grow impatient and frustrated. I feel a sense of connection among people who know mourning and longing. People who love despite what's been taken from or done to them. People who continue to bake bread, buy bread, and break bread with friends.

Give me nourishment. Let me live. Let me keep doing the simple things that define being human. Waking up. Seeing the light. Taking a sip of coffee. Toasting a piece of bread. Walking. Noticing a bird. Meeting eyes with a stranger and making them a friend. Cooking and eating and cleaning up—and doing it all over again. Trying. Failing. Triumphing. Washing the day away. Taking a sip of water. Making something from nothing. Feeling warmth. Touch. The moon. The breath. Drifting off to sleep.

When we live this way, enjoying these things, whatever we lose, or however we fail, can't take away the majesty of the blue sky. Can't rob us of the choice to connect. If we surrender, these things that happen can rub us smooth—take away our rough edges—polish us.

"Would you like to see the oven?" she asks. She has lost her parents, but still, "Would you like to see where the bread is made?"

The bread Ilan starts each day with in Paris. The bread he shares with his wife. With me. The sacred stash he will later share from the freezer when I visit him in San Francisco.

"Yes," we say. "Show us."

And we descend the stairs—four people who have lost and cried and been confused, but who are still certain of one thing.

Let's go on.

Let's look at the oven.

Let's break bread.

Together.

The Left

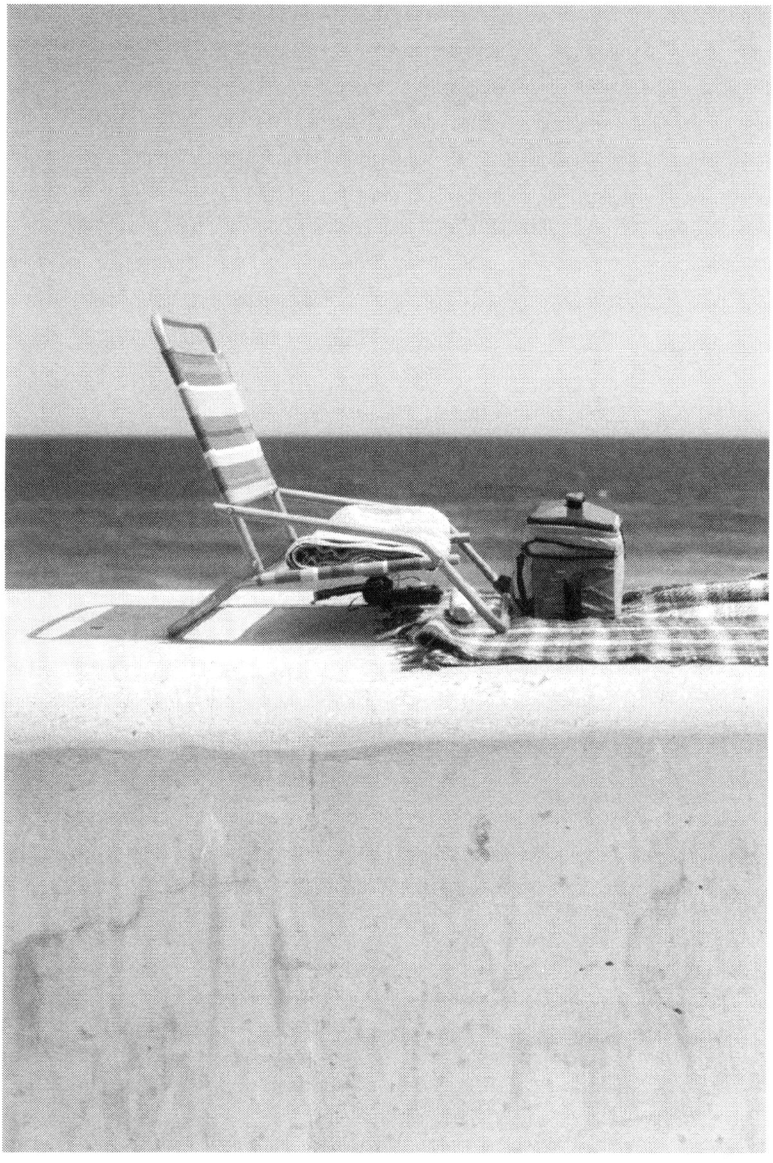

I woke up on a Saturday morning thinking about my thighs. I'd be wearing a swimsuit in front of another person later that day—and no swimsuit could conceal this part of the body. Board shorts aren't my vibe.

When puberty changed my form, my mother started to call me "TT"—*thunder thighs.* The other women in my family have skinny, strong legs, even when they're fat.

In college, my roommate said, "Nice cellulite." And my gay best friend, describing a guy he'd brought home, said that his lover's soft thighs, like mine, were an immediate turn off. I saw these comments as confirmation that this part of my body was unacceptable.

As I soldiered on into adulthood, I dragged my legs around like luggage—necessary, but a nuisance.

Then, when I was pregnant, I stood up one day and felt something in the skin on my legs give way. I could feel it ripping like worn-out denim. In an instant, I had hundreds of tiny stretch marks—little red and raw tattoos, scrawled across the front of my thighs. It was almost as if my legs, tired of being ignored, were screaming to be seen. Like the child who would rather have negative attention than no attention at all. Over time, they became scars.

So I was thinking about my thighs as I packed a bag for our breakfast on the beach. In the bag, I put in an avocado, crackers, cherries, a knife, and a parcel of Maldon salt for sprinkling. He was bringing the coffee.

A few days earlier, he'd emailed to say he was leaving the area and would like to see me. He suggested meeting on a private stretch beyond Napeague, nestled in between the celebrities in East Hampton and the hipsters in Montauk.

When I arrived, the ocean was rumbling. The sand was clear. I came prepared to dive in for my first swim of the year. We exchanged some texts to find one another. *Go to the left.* I'm already on the left.

We positioned our chairs. He took out a thermos of coffee and a container of oat milk. He had texted earlier that morning to ask how I would take mine. He poured one liquid into the other until I was satisfied with the proportions.

We met in a meditation group. He's smiley with big teeth. Silly. Present. I'm not the type of woman who thinks that men are noticing me. I appreciated his warmth but didn't interpret it as anything more than the kindness one expects from fellow meditators.

I held his cup for him while he filled it and then we talked, with the water as our witness. Every so often, my thoughts drifted to that inevitable moment when I'd have to take off the skirt I'd worn over my swimsuit.

"You didn't pick up on any of my cues," he said.

With his impending trip, there was no more time to leave words unspoken. And the ocean was creating urgency. I have left and been left enough times to know how to ride departures like waves. Jumping above certain ones, ducking under others. And yet some still manage to toss me around, twisting my neck, surprising me.

"I can be daft," I said.

"We could've spent the quarantine as lovers. I fantasized about you all the time."

"Really?" I asked, "What did you think about?"

The quarantine had been a creative but chaste time for me. There were many things produced. Words written. Meals cooked. Walks taken. Uncertainties. Dreams. But not sex.

"Well," he said. "It always starts with your thighs."

In younger years, I had been willing to internalize others' negative opinions about my body. So why not internalize this positive take? This was not about the male gaze. I wasn't forfeiting feminism. It was about seeing my thighs through someone else's eyes.

Maybe they were just fine.

I felt my perspective shifting. These thighs had a function. They pushed my baby out after 32 hours of labor. They propelled me through the 26.2 miles of a marathon. And they took me through the Camino de Santiago, a pilgrimage I walked in Spain after dropping Joe off at college.

I wonder how much time we collectively spend thinking about muffin tops, love handles, knock knees, cankles, bat wings, man hands, thinning hair, double chins, crows' feet, pendulous breasts, elevens, and thunder thighs. How many minutes? How many hours? How many days? Couldn't we have cured cancer or given someone undivided attention with all that mental energy? For me, it took half a lifetime of work and one conversation to release the loathing.

I dropped my skirt and walked to the shore. We went into the Atlantic. Into the water. Into the waves where we each had to find our own footing.

Then we said goodbye in the parking lot.

The next day, he was gone, driving west across the country. And I was left in bed. When I woke up, my thighs looked tan and beautiful against the white cotton of my slip. Things that are loved shape shift. Things that are loved transform. Things that are loved look different.

Letter to the Editor

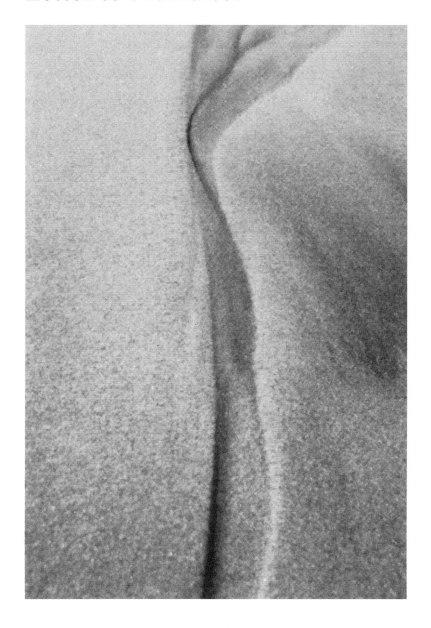

When Harry Met Sally is my favorite movie. I've seen it countless times, the first being on a date in the summer between my junior and senior years of high school. As a writer, I've read the script over and over. I quote lines with my best friend and am certain that the concepts in the film have informed my ideas about who I should be as a woman.

In her essay in *The Atlantic,* "The Quiet Cruelty of *When Harry Met Sally*" Megan Garber asks, is it better to be "low-maintenance"? Like Garber, I've spent most of the last 30 years aspiring to be an "L-M." But in the past few months, something shifted. In the Uber I took during a trip to Pittsburgh, my driver shared that he was going to marry his long-time fiancée. I asked him what he loves about her. His answer didn't include words like *nice* or *agreeable.* With a knowing grin that I could see in the rearview mirror, he said, "She has her own mind. She pushes back against things. She wants what she wants." And then, echoing that statement a month later, the gentleman who took care of my broken cell phone at an Apple Genius Bar declared that his wife was amazing because "she doesn't take crap from anyone."

I realized I had been wrong all along. I didn't need to limit my requests and keep my needs to myself. I needed to speak up more. Being an "L-M" doesn't make a woman lovable, at least not for these two men. Having a clear (kind) voice and using it to set boundaries seemed to make the difference. Sure, we all want to be accepted as we are, but we also want to be nudged beyond our limitations into bigger versions of ourselves.

Garber suggests that the central question of the film is not whether women and men can be friends but rather whether "a guy who hates almost everyone can open himself up to a single someone." I assert that, even if Harry first suggests that "low-maintenance" is ideal, that epithet doesn't describe *the single someone* he falls in love with. The one he's willing to chase across Manhattan in the middle of the night (because "when you realize that you want to spend the rest of your life with someone, you want the rest of your life to start as soon as possible"). Instead, the person he loves is someone who is willing to *want it the way she wants it.*

Perhaps Harry's personal evolution in the film is exactly the cultural evolution we've all been waiting for. Perhaps it heralds a time when women's opinions and desires are not shushed and shamed but rather invited, valued, and even celebrated with a coconut cake, chocolate sauce *on the side.*

On La Cienega

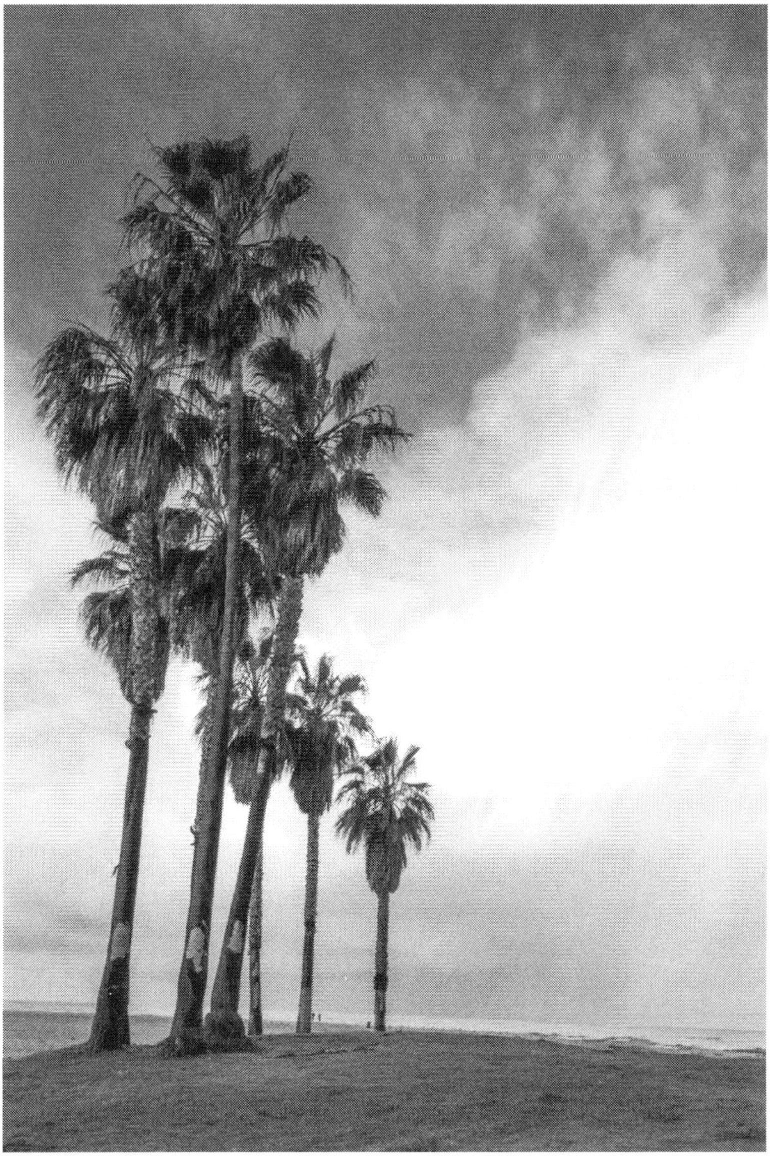

I knocked on my friend Donna's door in Van Nuys. She wasn't expecting me. No one in LA drives to the valley unless they have to, or they want good sushi, or they live there.

"Bella?" she said when she saw me. It was my nickname.

"He ended things," I said, struggling to get the words out before bursting into snotty sobs.

Two hours earlier, I'd been in West LA looking blissfully at the man next to me in bed. Both of us were naked. Then he opened his eyes and said "I can't do this." In time, I would come to understand that he wasn't "the one who got away," but losing him was excruciating. Later he would say that I was the closest he'd found to the right person, but that he knew he wasn't going to fall in love with me.

I couldn't begrudge him that. It was how I viewed myself: almost worthy of love but not quite. Childhood trauma, a poor body image, and being a single mother contributed to my feelings of shame and low self-esteem. I always felt I wasn't good enough to get the dream job, snag the soulmate, have the happy intact family, buy the house.

I seemed strong and believed women could do anything. Low self-esteem didn't stop me from becoming student body vice president. Becoming the first person with a Masters in my family. Being appointed clinical director of one of the first women's AIDS clinics in the country. Choosing to keep an unplanned pregnancy. And making more money than most men. But these feats were external—like medals—meant to prove something to myself and the world. Self-esteem has to happen on the inside. From within.

I read *Revolution from Within* by Gloria Steinem on a road trip to the Grand Canyon after I graduated college in 1993. By the time of that break-up in 2017, I'd been working on cultivating self-esteem for almost a quarter century. Now, thirty years after the book's publication, and over half a decade since I showed up on Donna's porch, the ubiquity of campaigns for "self-care" and "self-love" suggest that loving oneself continues to be a challenge for many women—and that it's the prerequisite to receiving anything we crave.

My sense of self-worth finally took hold decades after I first took a highlighter to Steinem's remarkable tome, and after many therapy sessions, 12-step meetings, and workshops. The time was 7:23am. A few months after my break-up, I was on the phone with Donna, driving on La Cienega somewhere north of Olympic and south of Beverly, surrounded by traffic and honking and beeping.

In Los Angeles, your car is not just a machine. Not just a vehicle meant to take you from point A to point B, or sometimes C and then back to B. It's an office. An extra room. A safe space. A womb. It's a place where problems get solved. Appointments made. Deals sealed. Where hard conversations happen. And sometimes a place of healing.

But I wasn't expecting a healing on that particular day in December of 2017. The big solar eclipse had already happened in August. I had run a 5K. Gotten a raise. Paid my bills, helped my kid apply to college. I'd been doing what I always did, not expecting anything extraordinary. I exited the 10 and made a left onto La Cienega and then pulled into the Starbucks drive-thru.

"Donna, hold on a sec," I said. She knew the drill. I ordered a medium dark roast with cinnamon powder and half-and-half, never remembering if the medium is a "Tall" or "Grande."

"Will that be all?" the voice from the speaker said.

"And egg white bites, please?" Ridiculous to say and yet I said it every day.

The details were rote. I knew them. Donna knew them. The woman at Starbucks knew them. I paid the six-something and made a right back onto La Cienega, continuing north to my West Hollywood office. That day, like all days, I drove in my perfectly clean emission-free car to my high-powered job, wearing a perfect outfit, having a perfect carb-free breakfast, arriving early. Yet not one of these attempts at perfection provided me with the sense of certainty in myself that I'd been hoping for. And I nursed the unfortunate conclusion that my lack of self-esteem must be a result of still having imperfections in my life.

Donna's voice came through the Bluetooth of my Prius. (I'd always called that car "my friend.") My morning talks with Donna usually covered things our teen kids were doing or (more often) failing to do. Sometimes recipes. I'm not sure how we got into a conversation about self-love that morning. But we did. And somewhere around the SLS Hotel, stopped by gridlock, she said something that struck me.

"If all we ever do is sit and put Maldon salt on toast together, that will be enough. You're not lovable for what you do, Bella. You're lovable for who you are."

It sounds cliché to say out loud. Even worse to write. I mean, *Duh*. And yet, at 44, I realized it had never really occurred to me. Lovable for who I am, not for what I do? Worthy of love *just because*? Unconditionally? Absofuckinlutely? With no evidence of being good or fixed or perfect?

Self-love is a birthright. Even Koko, the sign-language-speaking gorilla Steinem mentioned in her book, had self-worth. She described herself as a "queen" and a "fine gorilla person." But I didn't feel that way about myself.

Yet, there in the Toyota, something was shaking loose. The tired old notion that I needed to follow some perfect formula in order to be loved—that I needed to be anything but who I already am—was leaving. I had lived with my shame and unworthiness for a long-ass time. It was so much a part of me that it felt like my skin. And yet there it was, shedding. Coming off in one smooth sheath.

My eyes welled up as this simple truth filled my cells. I knew I'd never be the same again. I couldn't forget what I'd just felt. I might struggle plenty, but I could never feel unlovable in the same way again.

I opened the window and shook that skin off into the wind like a loose hair, to be run over on the pavement. A lifetime of unworthiness sent out onto La Cienega—you'd think it would've stopped traffic, created some kind of hold up, but no one even noticed.

I took a sip of coffee. Starbucks coffee never tastes *just right,* only good enough. And I was good enough, too. And good enough or not, I was worthy. I knew it.

Steinem had tried to tell me all those years ago, but I wasn't ready to take it in.

Maybe I should've realized this on my own—and sooner, for fuck's sake. But on that day in the City of Angels, Donna shone a light on a very simple truth that became undeniable and real, like a crystal flake of Maldon salt on my tongue.

I am loved. I am loving. I am lovable.

I left everything I'd thought was unlovable behind on the blacktop.

And when I think back to my copy of *Revolution from Within,* with its broken spine and loose pages and scribbles and highlighting, I feel grateful. The book planted seeds that I never gave up on, and that finally took root.

E Pluribus Unum

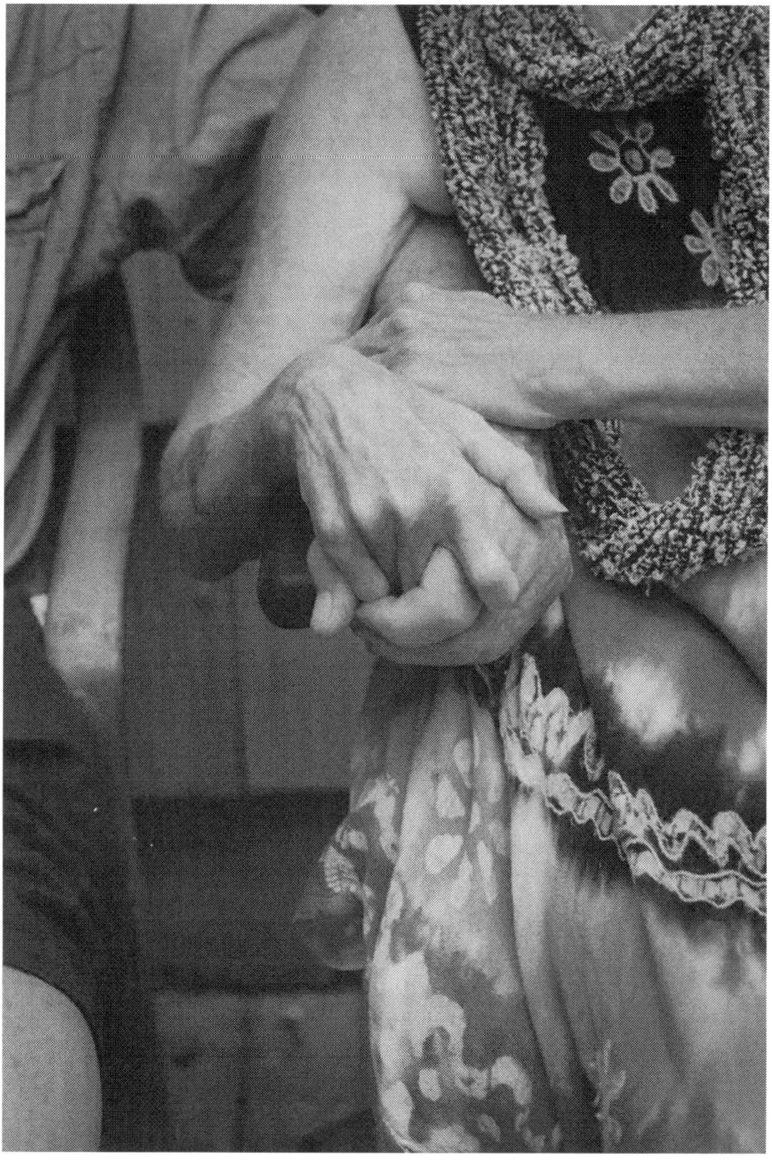

As we approach the anniversary of 9/11, I can't help but reflect on Thursday September 13, 2001, when I was called in as a crisis intervention counselor for the employees who worked at Windows on the World, the iconic restaurant at the top of North Tower.

Two days prior, many of the men and women I'd met with arrived at work to see the buildings on fire and people jumping out of windows. They all lost co-workers. They all lost their job sites. They all lost faith. Nothing in my clinical training at New York University taught me how to handle what was before me. Like so many other emergency responders, whether paramedics or firefighters or social workers, we were in unchartered territory.

On the Tuesday when the towers fell, I was living on the east end of Long Island with my one-year-old son. I immediately said yes when I got the call to come in and help. Due to bridge and tunnel closures, I couldn't get into Manhattan until Thursday, and the first thing I noticed was that, even amid tattered flyers with photos of the lost, there was a palpable sense of calm and cohesion on the streets. As a native New Yorker, it was something I'd never felt before.

I arrived at the location where I'd be counseling and met with employees in groups of twenty or more. People shared their stories. They listened to each other. What they'd seen. How they felt. The shock. The horror. The irreconcilable loss. I expected that. But what I didn't expect was this. As I was wrapping up the first group, an older woman spoke out.

"Before we go, can I say something?"

She looked around the room and was met with agreement, and so I let her lead. She stood up and reached for the hands of the people on either side of her. Almost as if by magic, separate individuals transformed into a circle where everyone was unified and holding hands.

"Let us remember those who lost their lives. Let us remember their families. Let us thank the nurses and doctors and rescue teams who are working tirelessly. Let us give thanks for our own lives. And, above all, may we be kind to one another."

This spontaneous circle of remembrance and gratitude happened at every group that day. Different leaders spoke different words, but the sentiment was the same.

The groups were diverse in every way, yet they didn't seem to care if the hand they held on either side of them belonged to someone of a different gender, a different race, a different religion, or a different sexual orientation. They didn't inquire into the person's political affiliation or immigration status. They didn't mind whether we were all talking to God, or G-d, or Allah, or Mother Earth. In those few days, in our unfettered fear and grief, we were the same. We were one.

Over these past years, and particularly through the global pandemic, I reflected on that Thursday. We are now so much more focused on what divides us than on what unites us. What happened? Why isn't a pervasive sense of empathy sustainable?

The United States is not even 300 years old. With the exceptions of the native people of this land, and the people brought here as slaves, many of us share a similar history—we are immigrants or children of immigrants. Either we were escaping something bad, hoping for better, or both. My mother and her family left Sicily to find opportunities after WWII, and my father's family came from Italy seeking help for his younger brother with Down Syndrome.

That day of crisis intervention counseling at a critical time in our nation's history humbled me. It was a concrete experience of the national motto—*e pluribus unum*—*out of many, one.*

That day I learned how to go on after, or amid, unthinkable tragedy.

We do it by standing together.

The Dog Shakes

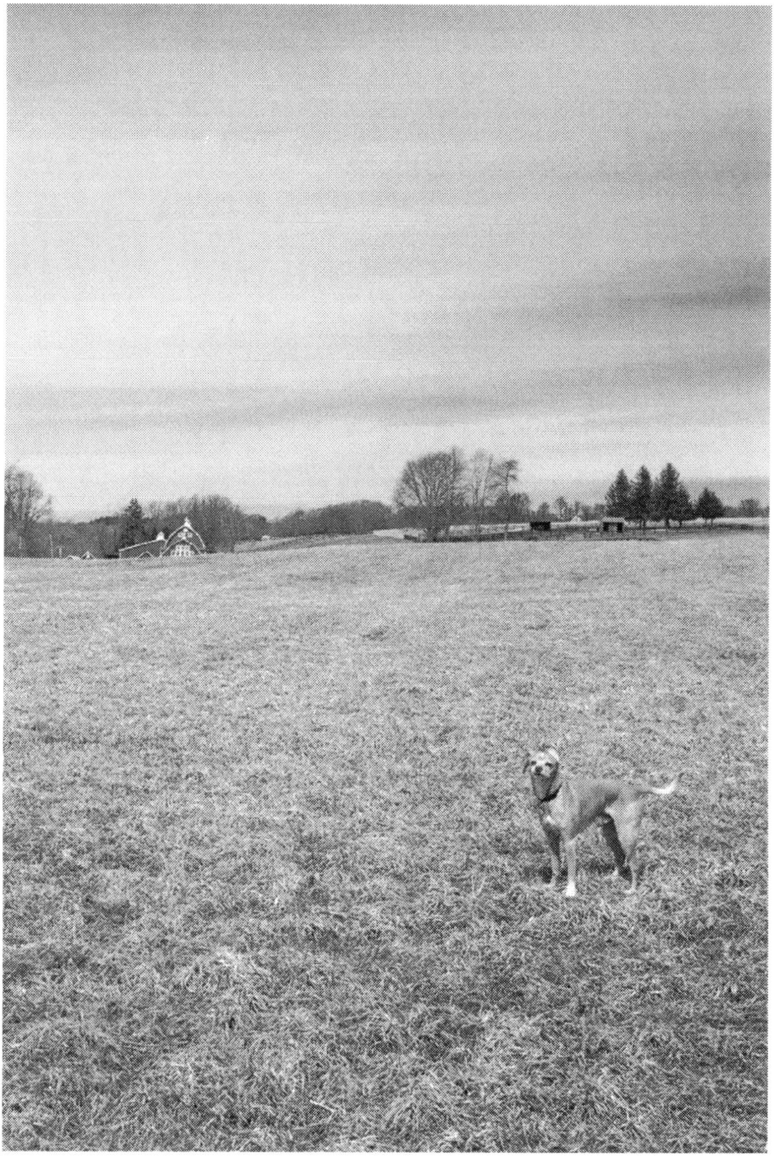

The sky is blue and cloudless through my apartment window on the Upper West Side. And the dog shakes. It's bright today. The autumn has changed the set design and lighting in the city. The sun is lower now and fills more of the room. I like it.

The leaves have changed, too. They're colorful. Each day a different landscape gets painted around the pool in Central Park right before my eyes.

And still, the dog shakes.

Does he shake because he's nervous? Is he helping discharge the panic of the pandemic in the city? In the world? Does he shake because he has a neurological condition? The vet says no. Maybe he's just a neurotic mess—plagued for this lifetime with endless anxiety except for the tiny moments of calm he finds basking in the sun on the street outside Bar Pisellino or sleeping under the covers.

We, too, are like this. Vibrating and stirring from one moment of calm to the next. Moving from one frenzy to another, with only small bits of respite in between. Traumas and the unpacking of them. Triggers and upsets. Misinterpreted words and text messages.

Are we even meant to be centered all the time? My friend says she's looking for enlightenment. To be able to always remember her true essence. To let her ego go for good.

But is that really what it means to be human? Or do we come here to muck it up?

Shake it up. Shake it off. Shake our leaves loose. Shake and shake.

Or, as a panhandler in Greenwich Village used to say while shaking his coffee can, "A whole lot of shaking going on."

The Bad Mother

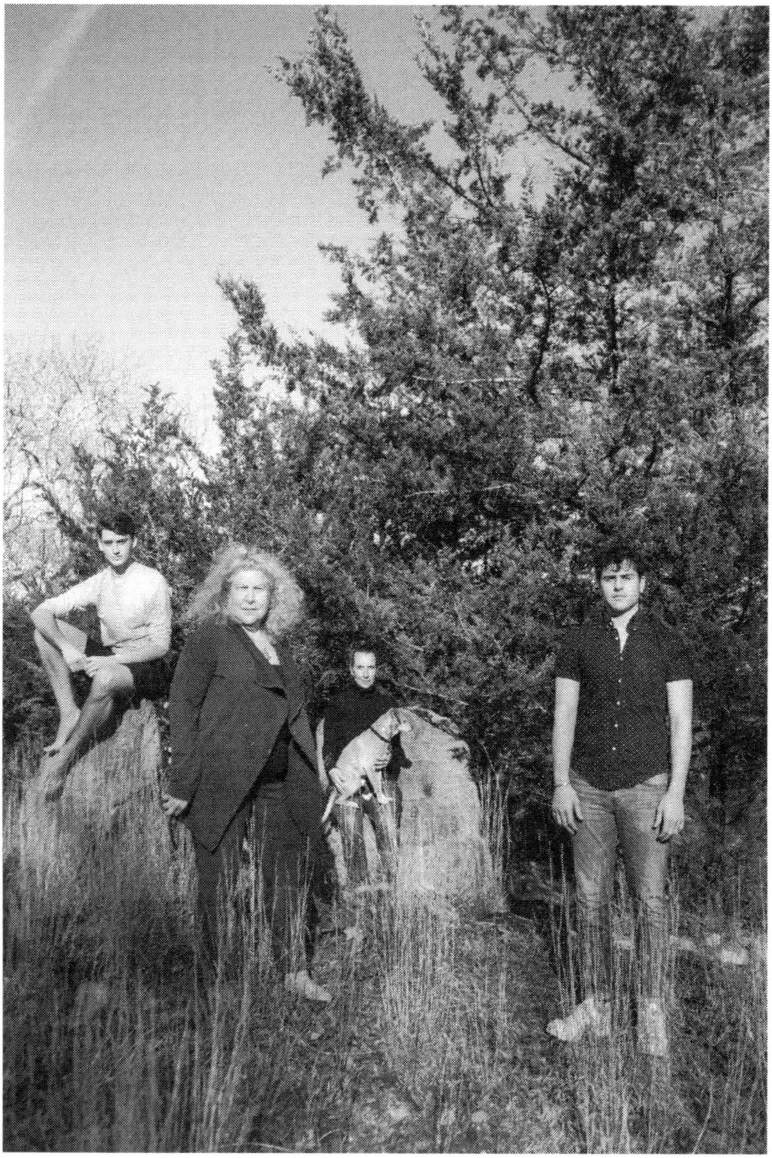

The spider plant sits on the console in front of the living room windows. Through the panes, one can see the southside of Central Park.

I received the plant as a gift from Lyuda, my only neighbor in Dover Plains — a small hamlet in Upstate New York. On an early spring day, she had asked me to help her harvest ramps. We used paring knives rather than pulling them out, to preserve the roots for the next year. I envisioned the meals I'd cook with them. When we finished, she invited me into her greenhouse to select a plant. One with spiky green and white-striped leaves beckoned. I took it home and placed it on the wooden island in the kitchen where it sat under the skylights. I placed a plate underneath to catch leaks.

Spring and summer passed, and my college-aged son, Joe, signed the lease on his first apartment in the Yorkville neighborhood of Manhattan. He was leaving the dorms but taking his roommate, Liam, along. The car got packed with mugs and art and dishes, and the spider plant got put in a cardboard box behind the driver's seat. At his place, it sat on the sunny kitchen windowsill, looking down into the air shaft of a fifth-floor walk-up. It lived there for many months. Most of the time, Joe remembered to water it.

But in mid-March 2020, Joe and Liam packed up their dirty laundry and laptops and came to my mother's house in Eastern Long Island, thinking it'd be only a week or two before they could return to their place. The headlines and sirens were freaking them out.

When Joe had graduated high school, we'd packed up our Santa Monica home, the place we'd moved into two days before he started kindergarten. Ninety-percent of our belongings got sold at yard sales or gifted to friends or, in the final days, carted off in pick-up trucks to Goodwill or the garbage. What remained still sits in a tiny storage unit in Upstate New York.

The plants were the hardest to leave behind. I never had a green thumb, but California living taught me to care for cacti, the botanical world's most forgiving creatures. The giant pots of succulents, which started off small and proliferated without any skillful tending from me, stayed on the stoop of our old place for the next tenant. The bonsais, which require more precision, got entrusted to someone who'd treasure them as much as we did.

During the packing process, I allowed Joe to keep more than I might have, a small concession to the fact that he wouldn't have a familiar home to return to during holiday breaks and summers. He labeled his boxes, "Important stuff... I guess." After I dropped him off at college in the financial district of New York City, I walked the Camino de Santiago in Spain alone, leaving my regrets on the path, reasoning that I had done the best I could as a single mother, forgiving myself for wherever I'd fallen short or failed, and hoping that someday I might get to make my amends with grandchildren.

I didn't expect that Joe and I would ever live under the same roof again, but there we were, with him sleeping in the next bedroom. Watching him taking classes on Zoom and eating every meal with him felt like getting to live one blessed extra day with someone dear who'd died. An unexpected do-over. And this time, I got to be a different kind of mother. Without the competing pressures of laundry, work, financial stress, creative aspirations, and romantic disappointments, I could be present and patient in ways I wasn't able to during Joe's childhood.

And not only did I get Joe, I got the bonus of Liam, too. I had always wanted more children but accepted that wasn't going to happen. Liam was the agreeable child I never got. The one who was eager to take the dog on a walk or go on a run with me, throw out the trash without a fight and do puzzles or crafts.

I was grateful when weeks turned into months, but I couldn't stop thinking about the abandoned plants in Joe and Liam's apartment and went to retrieve them. The succulents were fine, but the spider plant, dry and withered, seemed dead. I took it home anyway and cut away the leaves.

Joe and Liam finished their semester. We celebrated Joe's twentieth birthday with video messages played on a projector. The boys tanned in the backyard and swam in the bay. And after fifteen weeks, they returned to Manhattan. All of us transformed by our time together.

In July, after Joe and Liam were settled back into their own home, the spider plant announced its return, too, with bright green shoots. In Spanish, the spider plant is called *la mala madre*—the bad mother—for throwing her babies away, but each of the babies has the potential to grow into a whole new plant all its own. As with sourdough starter and love, the more you give away, the more there is for everyone.

Each of the original spider plant's dozens of babies got planted in tiny terracotta pots and given to friends, along with a printed-out story about second chances. Of death and resurrection. Of hope.

And the mother remains with me.

Confronting the Cold

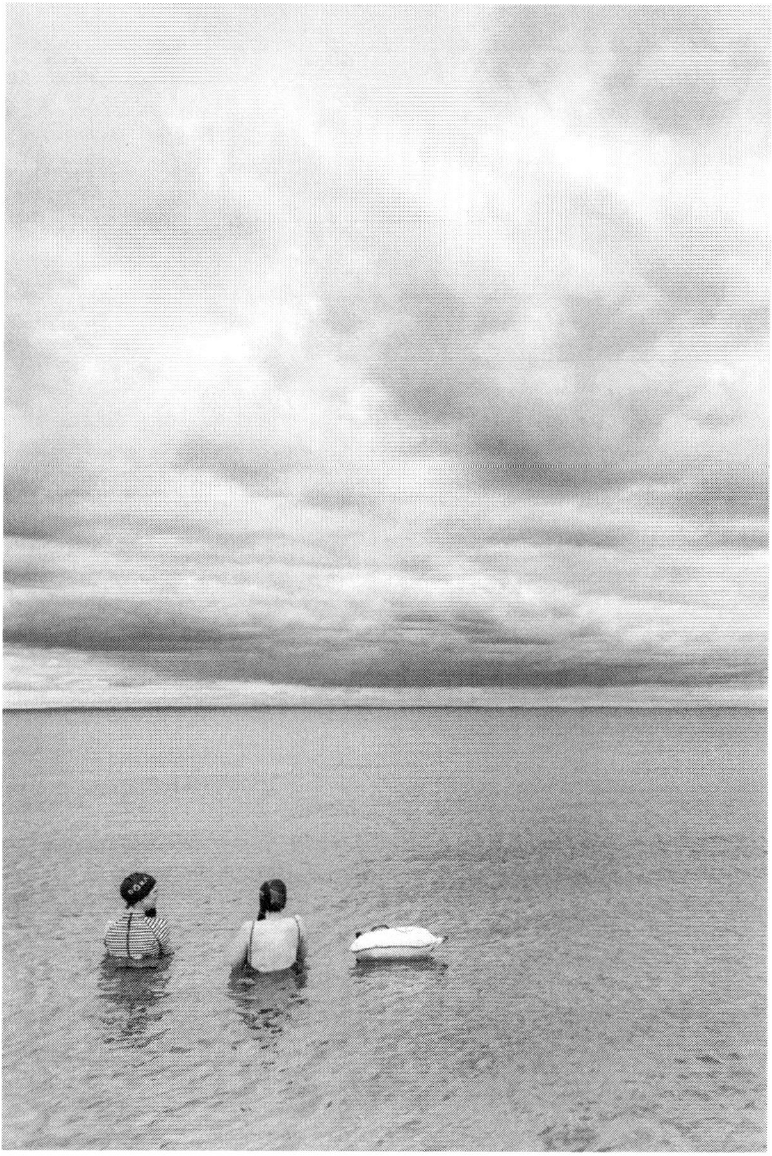

I park at Patricia's house. Today is the day I've planned to go into the Long Island Sound where East Marion meets the coast. Across the water I can see Connecticut. The sun has hidden behind clouds; despite it being early spring, the gray above us evokes the winter days we vowed to put behind us. The air temperature is 50. The water on April 17th is 40 degrees, not far from where it holds steady for most of winter.

I'm terrified, but it's too late to turn back. I'll disappoint the others. I'll disappoint myself. I hear my old therapist in my head with her heavy Israeli accent, "I thought you were done with martyrdom, Michelle?" My own voice says, "C'mon, it's just cold water."

This is not the first time I have done this to myself with fear. Talked myself out of something. Or tried to. And then attempted to scare the fear away with defenses and rationalizations.

It's only a conversation.
It's only a person.
It's only words on a white page.

And yet. And yet. And yet.

To understand what this day is for me, you must understand how afraid of the cold I am. It's not a rational fear. It's primal terror. I sleep with a heated mattress pad ten months out of the year. I use a down comforter in August. I travel with a hot water bottle. Getting into the water in summer during a heat wave isn't easy. I do it, but it requires some inexplicable sense of risk. So why am I doing this? What do I have to prove and to whom?

I consider possible past-life reasons for my fear. Death on the Titanic. Being abandoned in a snowy forest. Plane crashes in the arctic. The options are endless. It's not the water that scares me or the idea of drowning; I just don't like being cold. I go through current life possibilities, too: I was born in December. I was never placed on my mother's chest. I spent the first five days of my life alone in the nursery of the hospital where I was only held when nurses fed me. *Was I freezing then?* The fluorescent room must have felt so different from the dark, warm womb where I first grew—in spite of my mother's lifelong gastrointestinal issues, the racing of her anxious heart, and my parents' looping arguments. *Money. Jealousy. Blame. Betrayal. Shame.*

Lindsay, a photographer friend, was doing a series on winter swimmers and asked me to participate. I wanted to get over my fear. I committed in a non-committal way. Then, on Lindsay's Instagram, I saw other winter swimmers, but one stood out—Patricia. Statuesque. Elegant. Chiseled, balanced shoulders. Brown hair. Maybe forty or fifty. She swims 365 days a year. The photo Lindsay took of her winter swim showed her in a snow storm. Air temperature 18. Water temperature 30. She walked in without flinching. All composure. All contained. All cool. Cooler than the water itself. I want that. I want that kind of grace. I want that posture. I want that presence. But can I get it from cold water?

I followed Patricia's videos on Instagram, and each day something was imprinting on me. A longing to get in. I knew there was something for the water to teach me, but I didn't want to go alone. I had already done so much alone. Raised a child. Moved across the country and back. Walked the Camino. Made the only box of pasta in the cupboard after a business trip. Nursed a broken heart. Put toothpaste on my toothbrush each night. Bought my book in a bookstore when it was published. Crossed the finish line.

Alone. And alone. And more alone.

One day I sent a DM to Patricia: could I accompany you on one of your daily swims? The mentorship was more important than getting a record of the event on film. I'd ask Lindsay later about taking a photo. To my surprise, Patricia agreed. And this thing that had terrified me all winter now seemed intriguing. Enticing. Seductive. *Is it possible I don't have to do it alone? I can face this fear with someone by my side?*

Today, when I drive from East Hampton to Sag Harbor and get on the ferry to Shelter Island, and then on another ferry to the North Fork, I think about what I'd yell to my son Joe as I left on Saturday mornings for my long runs, back when I was training for the marathon. "I will succeed or I will fail, but I won't come back the same person."

Somehow this feels the same.

As I traverse the two forks of Long Island, south then north, a friend on the phone tells me about Wim Hoff and the way he befriended the cold water. At seventeen, he felt a sudden urge to jump into the frozen Beatrixpark Canal in the Netherlands. Later, the icy waters would help him overcome the sadness of his wife's suicide. As he developed techniques to face low temperature environments, he grieved and healed. I knew about Wim Hoff for many years—the ice man—but had never heard this story. Wim didn't know why he'd need the cold water when he took the plunge at seventeen, and I'm not sure what I'll learn about myself by stepping in, but I know I'll discover something. Only by putting ourselves in unfamiliar settings can we discover unknown parts of ourselves.

I drive by Patricia's house and have to backtrack. As I make a U-turn, I wonder to myself who I might be on the drive back. I'm forty-eight years old. My son is grown and going to be a senior in college. My career hasn't happened yet. I don't have a house. Or a partner. I notice picket fences and house numbers painted on planks of wood. Could this make a difference?

I'm early, so I stop far back in the driveway and close my eyes and try to still the stirring inside with meditation. As soon as I finish, Lindsay pulls in behind me. The timing worked out and she had agreed to take photos. We park side-by-side and start chatting. She's got cropped blond hair and is always wearing something rocker chic and cool. She has no interest in getting in the cold water, only capturing it on film. I don't look cool in borrowed ski pants and one of my father's old fleeces. Being a minimalist, I have pared down my winter wardrobe to almost nothing. I've known Lindsay since our sons were infants, but my nervousness about what's ahead overshadows my familiarity. Together, we walk to Patricia's house. And then Patricia, this person I've only seen on the tiny screen of my phone, becomes human before my eyes.

Most of the images of Patricia that I've seen have only shown me her back, as she strides into the water like a Greek goddess. Or like the fish who lived all winter below the ice of the pond in my house upstate. But in person, I can feel her warmth. She's sad about having to leave this house where she's lived for two years. She's not all strength; she's also softness—and then I remember that softness is, in fact, a part of strength. Am I not being soft enough with myself? Would it be okay if I didn't face this one fear? If I left it off my list? Accept that I don't like the cold and let that be that?

Patricia has already filled three bottles with hot water for us to drink after we get out of the sea. She explains it's important to bring our body temperature back up. The three of us make small talk, but there's anticipation lurking under the surface. We pack a bag with neoprene booties and gloves and thermoses. I end up carrying it. It becomes a joke: I'm being hazed. Lindsay adds camera equipment and boots to my already overstuffed straw bag.

We take the twenty-minute walk through the woods to the water's edge.

As we walk, these are the things I notice. There are no buds or leaves on the trees. Not yet. The wood is brown and winterized. Still. The sun is hiding somewhere. I have a quiet nature, especially when I'm in the woods, but today I talk more than usual. My fear materializes into words. Nonsense. Stories. Chatter. The only color is the bright yellow forsythia that has just bloomed. Like Patricia, it's not afraid of the cold. Even before the jonquils and daffodils appear, it blazes like golden light. There is also the red jacket. The maroon hat. The orange buoy. The marigold straw bag. And then there is the water. Clear and turquoise and green and then clear again. Patricia had warned that it can be choppy in this spot, but now it's calm and gentle. Not angry or agitated. As I'd seen the softness in Patricia, I now see it in the water, too. She is meeting me and my fear with kindness. Not something to be conquered or plunged into, but perhaps asking to be seen in a new way.

We find a log where we can leave our shoes and clothes. Hats and gloves and boots. It's Patricia's usual dressing spot near Mermaid Rock. She tells me the order in which to take my clothes off so that I don't get too cold. Once your thighs are exposed, your body temperature plummets, she explains, so we take our pants off last. I cover my head with a cap. She does the same. I tuck her hair in. It's brown and chin length. This two-dimensional creature from Instagram is now incarnate in front of me. Real. Alive. Breathing. We are in this together.

We're wearing only our swimsuits now, bathing caps and surf gloves and booties. I feel equipped. Suited up. Armored and bare at the same time. We approach the water's edge. Patricia's voice lowers. It's a whisper. A gentle lapping wave. A prayer.

Patricia tells me that she announces her full name to the water and asks for permission before going in. And so, I do the same.

"My name is Michelle Carmela Fiordaliso. May I enter?" The water remains still.

"Yes, you can enter. Yes. Come in." I'm surprised when the sea answers, but she does. And so I approach with my hands still in prayer position. I take a step. And then another. And another. I stop. Patricia does the same beside me. I feel tentative and vulnerable.

"It's okay if we only make it to our shins," she says.

"It's okay if we just feel the water," she says.

"It's okay," she says.

She's here with me. Like I know the water is here with us both.

I believe Patricia when she says she won't mind if we've come all this way only for me to dip my covered toe in. It's nice to wear booties, because I don't feel the rocks. I don't like sleeping in socks, but I like this. Then the skin on my calves meets the sea. My hands are still in prayer position. "Yes, it's cold," I acknowledge to my body. "You're okay. We're okay." I feel the cold, but this cold I feared so much is manageable. I can meet it where it's meeting me.

Patricia glances over at me. I'm in her terrain. She's comfortable here. I'm the novice, but I don't feel like an imposter. I don't want to run. To flee. To escape. I'm working this out. And as I meet the water, I meet my cells—my selves. The selves that can seal the deal. Sell the book. Buy the house. Get the guy. Or do none of those at all and still be okay at the end of the day. But I'm not there. I'm here. Present. And the rest of the world falls away. I don't think about Lindsay on the shore taking photos. I forget she's there. I don't think about my life. I don't think about the dramas that plagued me on the drive over. The work projects. The getting it wrong. The *I-don't-know-hows.* I don't think — period. It's a relief not to hear words in my head. Crafted sentences. To-do lists. Desires. Static. Songs. Bits of dialogue.

I remember what Patricia told me on the walk over. *You can give anything to the water. She will take it all. Nothing scares her.*

I remember giving my sorrows to the sand on Kauai a few years back. Lying there with my belly on the beach, I asked her to take anything I no longer needed. She said to give it to her. Give it all to her. Everything. I was reluctant. *Are you sure? There's ugly stuff in here!* I heard a cackling laughter. *Are you kidding? I'm born of volcanoes—anything you give me I can incinerate in a second.* And so I did. I gave it all to her. My unfinished projects. My unsold scripts. My insecurities. My cellulite. My brokenness. My herniated L5-S1. My wrongs. My rejections. My regrets, few as they are. My unlived moments. My untrained dog.

And here I am in the opposite of that fiery island in the Pacific—the polar freeze of the Atlantic.

I ask the sea to take anything that remains. Anything dragging me down. Preventing me from flight. Anything at all. And as she does my eyes well up. It's leaving me. All of it. Liquifying beneath me and all around me. Disintegrating. Dissolving. I feel fluid.

Patricia looks at me. I imagine that if I weren't here she might be swimming or doing something different, but she seems patient and willing to bear witness to exactly where I am. To be nearby. I often keep my mind on others. *Do they have what they need? Are they content? Fed?* But I don't worry about whether this experience is satisfying for her.

"Are you in pain?" she asks.

We've been in the water for almost fifteen minutes. I realize my face must be contorted in some way. I realize there are tears welling up in my eyes. I realize I don't want her to worry.

"No," I say. I'm grateful.

My gaze pans from left to right. Connecticut is a wide vista. The water is crystalline. The clouds above us are moody and dramatic. A horizon has been scientifically proven to soothe human beings. We seek them out. When I think about being grounded, I think about feeling the earth under my feet. Sand on my belly. Grass beneath me. But someone once told me that we are even more grounded in the water because we are in the earth— not on her surface but inside her. Now I am part of the horizon, too.

"Do you want to try putting your hands in?" Patricia asks. I look down and see that my hands are still in prayer position.

"Yes," I say.

I follow her lead and release my hands from their position. With the prayer already said, I swirl the water. Stirring. Caressing. Getting to know this element from the inside out.

I am small. I am vulnerable. I am unsure of myself and totally certain at the same time.

"Do you want to go under?" she asks.

"I do," I say without hesitation.

I dunk my head below the surface, and the cold touches my face and then engulfs me. It is crushing. Numbing. And yet, it also makes me come alive. I realize extremes can do that. Migraines. Childbirth. Grief. Longing. A 124-degree day in Palm Springs did it once. I welcome the water's touch. Cryotherapy. Somehow this baptism seems like something that should be done in triplicate, and so I dunk myself two more times. I want to be covered from toe to head in the icy water. To leave the last bits of me behind—what they are, I'm not exactly sure. Maybe it's the part that thinks it's foolish to hope that I will break through—and then I do—I break the surface of the water and am part of the horizon again.

It's time to return to the shore. I'm not in a rush to get out, but I take Patricia's cues, and we go. It feels good to be led. Lindsay directs us and takes a few photos on film with a Bronica of the two of us standing on Mermaid Rock. More humble than triumphant. Like hard bread soaked in water during wartime, I'm softened, not tough.

Standing on the sand again, I am the same. I am different. Patricia takes a towel and dries me off the way I've watched nurses towel newborn babies to get their temperature up. She dries my neck and back while I remove my wet bathing suit and put on pants and other layers. She tells me that I need to get dry and stay warm now that I've left the water.

We haven't said much, yet I feel an intimacy. I've entrusted Patricia to see more of me than people who've known me for decades. We often underestimate the power of witnessing.

I barely know the cold wintery water but I feel this connection with it now and I barely know Patricia but I have let her take care of me. To mother me. To nurture me in ways I rarely have been. Ever. I let few come so close. To see me. My edges. My fears. My imperfections.

When we make our return trip to Patricia's house, I'm quiet. Meditative. Insular. Patricia makes me a cup of tea. She and Lindsay chat, but I don't feel like participating.

"May I use the bathroom?" I ask.

"Of course, either one," she says.

I pick the small one downstairs and sit on the toilet. My body feels like it's doing something. Warming itself up. Searching for homeostasis. Equilibrium. I put my hands down on the tops of my thighs and my skin is cold to the touch. There are nice soaps on the window ledge. Everything smells good. I wonder when I will live in a home again. One where I have placed every item and eliminated all the ones I don't love. But I don't attach my worthiness to this. Not now. I feel complete. I hear voices but don't make out words. I am aware of water. Liquid coming out of me and in the bowl beneath. And then pouring out of the faucet as I wash my hands.

When I walk back into the room, over Lindsay's shoulder, I see a couple of snaps from the day on her iPhone. I notice the size of my thighs and the dimpled skin that covers them, more pronounced in the glaring light of day. My back looks rounded instead of long from my hands being in a prayer position. I know the images will be posted on Instagram and I'm embarrassed by how easily this transformative moment has been highjacked by self-consciousness. *Aren't I beyond this—this relentless judgment of my able body, my healthy body, my body made even more extraordinary by the day's events? This superficial scrutiny. This vanity.*

I want to look as graceful and humble and whole as I feel inside. Yet the picture doesn't match the feeling I have, and it saddens me. I guess there is more to give to the sea. So much more to surrender. I judge myself for judging myself, and that judgment bothers me.

On the drive home, I hold these two realities.

The way I have overcome something. The way the sea is now available for swimming, not just in summer, but any day of the year. The way I can meet whatever I'm faced with—even the cold, especially the cold.

And that makes me remember that I can meet this resurfacing of shame, too. These old beliefs and voices that say I have to look a certain way to be loved. The thoughts that wash in: *Of course Patricia has a partner who's painting their new house for her; she's a gorgeous warrior-woman.*

It's not either/or. The accomplishment or the shame. It's *and.* It's both. I struggle to find a place to put these polar opposites. Expansive and contracting. Fearless and terrified. Healed and still more to be healed, for as long as this earthly body breathes. Ugh.

A couple of weeks later, I end up on an unexpected trip to Mexico.

After two taxis, a plane trip, a ferry, and an ATV ride, I arrive at the water's edge.

The gulf is clear and turquoise and over eighty degrees. I approach it like Patricia taught me, with care, with prayer, with presence. I take her voice with me to Holbox Island, a tiny slip of land off the north coast of the Yucatan Peninsula. I can't unfeel what I felt that day in the cold water. Unsee what I saw. Unknow what I knew. The water is different now.

This sea holds me with tenderness. It's sublime. Divine. Standing in this warm womb-like water, I see that the water, like me, is both healing and destructive. Both infinite (covering the earth) and scarce (in a drought). Tempestuous and taciturn.

All this comes into focus as my feet sink into the silky sand. Having gotten into cold water, I understand this warm water better. I understand myself better, too.

I accept that, like the water, I am all things.

The deep and the surface.
The beautiful and the ugly.
The buoyant and the drowning.

The Sideboard

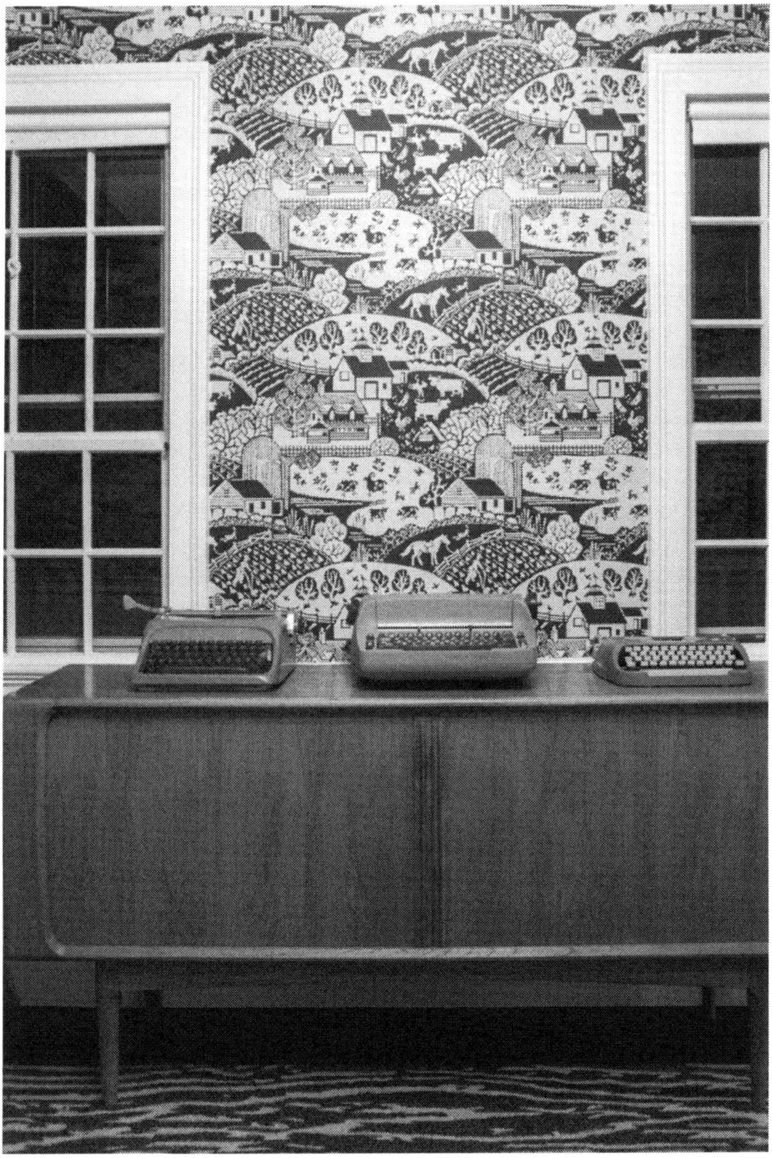

Nothing could've prepared me for what it would be like to live in the golden light of California. Visiting didn't provide a clue; to know that light, you have to live in it. Bask in it. Bathe in it. Watch it when you're up too early at sunrise and witness how it changes throughout the day and at different parts of the year. How it looks after a storm. From inside your car. Under Jacaranda trees in bloom. All this can't be accomplished on a visit.

To know the light, you have to live in the light. And we did. For 13 years.

The night before we left New York, we had dinner at a friend's house. Joel said, "I give you six months. Six months and you'll be back." By the time we returned more than a decade later, he was dead and gone. Esophageal Cancer. 66.

We took a plane to Los Angeles. But when our time there was done, we drove back east. It seemed too easy to be air-lifted out of a place where we'd set down roots for so long.

I remember the day I went to the valley to buy our sideboard. I found it on Craig's List. I used to say, "Craig's List is G-d's way of getting me shit since he doesn't do direct delivery." This console was the thing that set our house apart. I often envision a focal point in a room. It's how I decorate.

I thought I'd have to settle; the pieces in the stores were too expensive. I'd have to make do with something from Ikea—something functional, not special. But there it was. The ad read, "Oak Sideboard—$200." The seller didn't know what he had. Something like this usually went for around $3000. It's teak and mid-century modern and has hand-crafted rolling doors. It was meant to be a part of our family, and I was going to bring it home.

"I'll give you $235 if you hold it," I said to the guy on the phone.

I drove deep into the heart of the San Fernando Valley. No GPS. No Thomas Guide. No real idea where I was going. The prized piece of furniture fit in the back of my new Subaru Outback. The two of us made the drive back to Santa Monica, and gardeners on my street helped carry it in for 20 bucks.

Over the years, my son and I slept in all three bedrooms in that apartment. We changed the direction of the kitchen table. But that piece stayed where it was. Steady. Solid. My friend Faina helped me change the art over it. We put a gallery of pictures and paintings together that lasted longer than she did. By the time we left LA, she was gone, too. Lupus. 42. I wonder if embedded in the fibers of the wood are words from that mundane and magic conversation we had about nails and frames and perfect placement.

When my son and I moved away, we left most of our stuff behind. Pick-up truck after pick-up truck left full from our yard. Who knows where those pieces ended up. In which houses or landfills. Who uses them now? We drove back east. After a stint in the safety of Charlie's garage, that piece followed months later on a moving truck—delivered to upstate New York in a snow storm. I placed it in the empty middle room.

Then, when I left that house, my brother helped me carry it out and set it down in a storage unit where it sits alone today, waiting for its next home. It was a long journey that changed Joe and me. But the piece of furniture remained the same. We are different for having gone. For having lived in that light for so long. From here, it feels like a dream. Long but fleeting at the same time. Yet we each have friends and former lovers who can confirm we were there.

We didn't just visit.

We didn't imagine it all.

We lived it.

Choose Stars

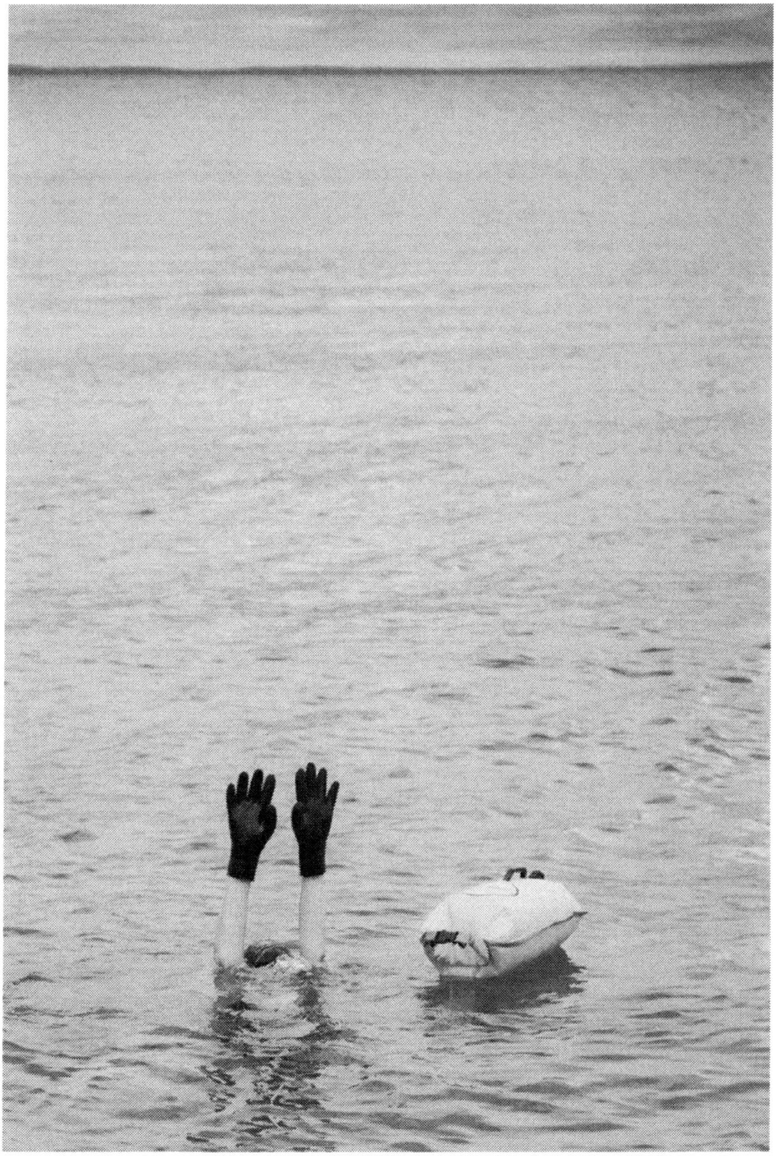

Five of my close friends would die in a year. Two already had. I was in a deep depression, sleeping too much and hiding in the bathroom at work to cry. Facing irreconcilable losses, I decided to take a Shaman-guided psychedelic journey in the California desert. It felt like a last resort.

I knelt before the beautiful Shaman, her long hair flowing behind her.

"How deep do you want to go?" she asked.

"Deep," I said.

"How does your body respond to psychedelics?"

"I don't know. I've never taken them."

With that, she determined how much of the brew I should imbibe, measured it into my cup, and placed the cup in my hands. The liquid was a blend of the vine and leaves that make up Ayahuasca, a hallucinogen from the Amazon that contains the chemicals DMT and MAOI. When ingested, it can produce experiences similar to those described by people who've died and come back to life: a new sense of purpose, a clear view of the matrix, a profound connection to love— source — God.

I had no idea what I'd get, but I knew I needed something. I was desperate.

My friends who were dying weren't old; they were in their 40s and 50s and 60s. Lupus, ALS, cancer, cancer, more cancer. After the second death, I found myself in a low place, but it wasn't for the reason one might expect. I wasn't full of grief but of envy. Why did they get to be done with the hard work of being alive? When could I do the same?

Ram Dass described death as "taking off one's tight shoe," and I wanted to be barefoot. I had the very thing my friends all desperately wanted—more days on this great green earth—and yet I wasn't interested.

Nothing was wrong. In fact, things had never been more right. At 43, I had a teenage son I loved fiercely; my Santa Monica home was a haven; my work as an executive coach was meaningful and brought in enough money to alleviate the financial burdens that had dragged me down for most of my life. I had a wonderful community of friends. And, having just finished producing and directing a documentary that would go on to win six awards, I felt creatively fulfilled.

But my life felt like a book I was tired of reading. I wanted to give up on page 103 and return it to the library, and that concerned me. There had been times in my life when desperate circumstances had made me want to die, but this was different, because things were good. Yet it felt more meaningless than ever. I couldn't live another forty years feeling like that.

It was around that time that a friend told me about his experiences with Ayahuasca.

"I felt my ego and identity fall away. I got a glimpse of what's really important," he said.

I put his tales of transformative epiphanies in my back pocket and tried to address my symptoms as signs of clinical depression and complicated grief. I also went to the doctor and found my thyroid medication needed adjusting. Increasing my dosage did make some difference. I no longer needed to sleep in the afternoons. Blood work showed my Vitamin B levels were pathologically low, and correcting them stopped the uncontrollable crying. I changed my diet. Got acupuncture. And talked with loved ones and therapists about the dear friends I'd lost and the others who were dying. But the flat feeling wasn't going away.

Ayahuasca wasn't popular at the time and I didn't know what a journey would be like, but I knew I didn't want to try it when my teenage son was around. Then I learned about an upcoming ceremony that coincided with dates when he'd be performing an opera in Edinburgh. So I signed up, and things fell into place. I took two days off from work. A friend offered to drive me to the desert, stay in a nearby hotel and pick me up the following day. And there was enough time to start the *dieta,* a three-week diet that eliminates processed foods, alcohol, sugar, and meat to prepare the body.

An Ayahuasca journey can last from eight to twelve hours, so it typically happens overnight. On the show *Weeds,* Nancy Botwin's drug dealer says, "Peyote's a bicycle; Ayahuasca, a rocket ship." I'd had little experience with mind-altering substances, but I was ready and willing to take the ride. It was crisis, not curiosity, that led me to seek out this kind of help. I was scared of tripping, but far more frightened that my state of mind would stay the same.

I shared my plan with only a couple of friends. I didn't want my mind fogged with others' fears; nor did I want anyone to point out that this was out of character for me. I'd smoked pot for the first time after graduating college, on the day Kurt Cobain killed himself, and there hadn't been many times since. I'd taken ecstasy a couple of times while clubbing at The Tunnel in the 90s. I rarely drink alcohol. I'd always been responsible with substances, and single parenthood made me even more so. But this wasn't meant to be an escape. It was an attempt to move towards, not away, from something. What that something was, I couldn't yet name.

Ceremonies normally involve twenty-five to thirty attendees, but mine was on a Monday, and there were only five of us. I liked it better that way. I'm a caretaker by nature, and the idea of too many tripping people overwhelmed me. When I arrived, I set up my "nest" with plenty of space around me—blankets and pillows, my journal (not realizing that writing would soon become an impossible task), lip balm, eye drops, and a change of clothes. Everything I needed.

We were each given a bucket and bandana, because vomiting is common. I hate vomit. Having worked in hospitals as a social worker on the AIDS unit, and as a doula with laboring women, I've seen a lot of birth and death. Bodily substances like blood, milk, phlegm, and feces are not a problem for me. But vomit is.

The yurt where the ceremony took place was a fabric dome. It had air-conditioning piped in. It was comfortable and cozy. We sat in a circle with plenty of space between us. The other attendees and I took turns setting intentions. I told them that I wanted my disinterest with life to go away. I talked about my friends dying. One woman had just lost her father, and a man had lost his husband. It seemed that death and grief had caused many of us to seek out this unusual solution. I think that's because, as a culture, we demonize this very normal part of being human. We deny that death can be a gift and turn away from it at any cost.

"My intention is to have access to joy," I said. "I want to re-engage in life. Maybe even engage like I never have before."

The lights were dim, and the Shaman chanted and sang. I drank my dose. It was disgusting, bitter, brown and sludgy. Unlike anything I'd ever tasted.

I waited, not feeling anything. Then, as I looked at my hands in front of me, I realized that something *was* happening: my hands were changing. They looked tiny and childlike and then old and wrinkled. Sometimes the left one grew bigger than the right.

Hands are important to me. They are the part of my body I like best. My hands are unique in that they're large for a woman but also very delicate and bony at the same time.

"You could've been a hand model," a friend once said. "Twenty years ago."

Another reason hands are important to me is that I play Mahjong. In the game, you have to make a specific spread with the tiles you receive. It's called a "hand." A strong player can change their hand mid-game; at the time, I really needed to change my life's hand. Just because the challenges of my existence had so far encouraged me to play the hand of victim, martyr, caretaker or hero didn't mean I had to play those roles forever. I could change my hand mid-game, mid-life.

Ayahuasca seemed to know exactly the way to speak to me so that I'd hear. It drew out things from my subconscious that would carry the most meaning for me. The message about changing hands came through loud and clear. But what was even louder was the woman vomiting in the yurt beside me. It sounded like a tsunami of puke was emerging from inside her.

"Do you like that?" I heard a voice say.

"Uh, no, no I don't like that."

"Why not leave? She's on her journey — you're on yours."

I could dialogue with the voice I was hearing.

I didn't wonder whose voice it was. I didn't care if it was God or my higher self, but I was aware that I could speak with it. It hadn't yet occurred to me that I could leave the yurt, but after that conversation, I picked up my bucket and bandana and headed outside, where I lay down in a fetal position on the desert floor wearing only a white linen dress. The air had cooled, and I was aware of the sand below me but not of my other surroundings.

Soon the nausea started building up, and I reached for my bucket. I felt my stomach tumble and my throat tighten.

"You can do this through sickness, or you can do it through stars. Keep in mind that one option is not better, but choose," I heard the voice say.

I looked up at the desert sky. The stars were numerous and clear. I hadn't noticed them before, but now the choice seemed obvious. Who would choose sickness over the cosmos?

"I choose stars," I said out loud. And as if by a magic spell, the nausea subsided. While it did, I traveled through the constellations I knew and discovered ones I'd never known before.

This happened over and over. The nausea would appear along with the same directive. "Sickness or stars. One is not better, but choose. Choose. Choose." Each time I chose stars, the nausea reliably disappeared.

The cycle continued five or six times until something struck me. We're here on earth to learn. Simple but often impossible lessons like connection, presence, self-acceptance, forgiveness, and love. We can learn these lessons through sickness, betrayal, bankruptcy, abandonment, addiction, shame. Or we can learn them through wonder, nature, art, sex, food, music—what the voice was describing as "stars." We can choose to learn through beauty rather than pain.

I'd been choosing the hard path for so long. But, lying there under the night sky, I realized I could start learning through delight. The lessons are no better when learned through strife. I had always taken pride in my grit, but being tough had grown boring. I didn't need to put my focus on the pain.

Choose Stars: this was a book about life that I wanted to keep reading. This was a book I could read for the next forty years. The joy that had eluded me came into focus. I dozed on my sleeping bag in the yurt, wondering if I would remember any of it in the morning. To my surprise, I did. I woke up as the sun was rising and wrote down every detail, every word of dialogue that I'd heard, all the anecdotes and stories that had bubbled up from my subconscious. It was as if I'd been given an enchanted set of encyclopedias. *Change your hand mid-game. Don't carry other people's guilt and shame. Be present and open. If you don't like a role, stop playing it. Feel everything.* And most importantly, *choose stars.*

My friend Charlie picked me up, and we went to have breakfast in the tiny town. While he'd been watching TV in a hotel, I'd been dissolving into the universe. It was hard to explain, but he said that I looked different. Brighter. And I was very hungry. I felt good in a way that I had rarely felt. Not high. Not elated. Just in my body. Heart in my heart. Feet in my feet. And those feet firmly planted on the ground. I was grateful to be alive and eager to go forward.

As we drove the three hours back to Santa Monica, I wondered if the feeling would last a day or a week. Maybe a month, I hoped. It's lasted for over eight years now. From that day forward food tasted better. Sex became more connected. The light through the trees looked different. I allowed myself to feel the depth of my love for my son without holding back. There's still pain and heartbreak. Disappointment and frustration. But where I put my focus has shifted and that has made all the difference. The milestones matter so much less, and the small moments matter so much more. Life hasn't been perfect, but I have felt healed and whole.

In the months after my Ayahuasca journey, three more close friends died. People who had taught me so much about life and love were leaving the world. But the experience I'd had in the desert didn't numb me like I feared it would. Quite the opposite.

On the day my dear friend Annette died, I walked into her hospital room. She held my hand and looked into my eyes.

"How's this going to go down?" she asked.

"You'll take a breath, and then another, and at some point you'll dive into the wildness."

"Today?" she asked.

"If you want," I said.

We sang, and I held her. We talked and joked. I felt it all. The fullness of those last moments I had with her in physical form. How very much I loved her. And when she was gone, I wailed.

My love and loss swelled like a wave in the days and months that followed. Sometimes it still does now. And when it does, I welcome it, because I know it means I loved her and that the love lives on.

Acknowledgments

Working as a freelance writer requires the support of fellow writers. I'd like to thank the members of my longtime writing group, where I first read some of these essays and lots of other things: Nicole Haimes, Annie Jacobsen, Kirston Mann, Annette Murphy, and Sabrina Weill. I'd also like to thank my current drop-in writing group, including Kevin Jacobsen, Erica Rosenast, Rob Stark, and David Wilzig.

Thank you, Tara Ellison, for supporting my writing; submitting and getting rejections (and occasionally acceptances) on a daily basis; and editing, bantering, and sending funny memes.

Charlie Peters, for editing my work and always supporting my creative journey, whether by building me a desk or by co-writing together or daily "Connections."

Kirston Mann (again), for always being a creative companion in painting, writing, and life.

Chloe Hsu, for the cover art and for knowing how to make collaboration a joy.

Abby Rosebrock, for stellar editing.

Lindsay Morris, for letting me pair my pen with your eye.

To the ones who keep me aligned and lit up: Rebecca Jurkevich, Adelaide Mestre, Mimi Fuenzalida, Michele Lynch, Deborah Jacobson, Gabriela Bohm, Sam Souccar, Sam Salameh, Joseph Ariel Towne, Robyn Brown, Nicky Carbone, Jessica Porter, Brian Eng, Elisha Wiesel, Lynn Bartner, Laurel Lobovitz, Ilan Kinori, Dorana Jurkevich,

Susie Theodorou, Laurie Klatscher, Kathleen Tripp, Jed Simon, Olga Berwid, The Puglia Pod, WhatsApp Love, Villa10 Love, and the Santa Monica Kibbutz.

To my mother, father, Sandy, Robert, Denise, Danielle and Stephen for your love and support.

Thank you to my friends and family, who make everything mean something better and who tolerate me alchemizing our experiences into stories.

For Percy, my starter husband, who taught me secure love.

And to my son Joe, for always being a champion of my words. You say, "I went to sleep every night to the sound of my mother's typing fingers." And I'm a notoriously aggressive typist. That couldn't have been a soothing way to drift off to sleep. You are the most thoughtful, spirited, big-hearted person I know. I love you. Joe/Joy—same difference.

Index of Photos

In order of appearance

Michelle Fiordaliso

Photo Credit: Cory Rice

Michelle Fiordaliso is an author, essayist, and screenwriter who started her writing career as a playwriting fellow at Uta Hagen's HB Studio and was the recipient of a PEN Center USA award for literary fiction. Her work has been published in *The New York Times, The Los Angeles Times, Chicago Tribune, Ms.,* and *The Washington Post.* The non-fiction break-up book she co-wrote, *Everything You Always Wanted to Know About Ex*, established her as a relationship expert on *Today, KTLA* and *Oprah Radio* with Gayle King. For more information, visit https://michellefiordaliso.com/ or follow @ michellecarmelafiordaliso.

Lindsay Morris

Photo Credit: Self-Portrait

Lindsay Morris is a photographer known for documenting events in her personal life and surrounding community. She is a 2023 TED speaker and a regular contributor to *The New York Times,* including two *New York Times Magazine* cover stories. Her work has been featured in renowned publications and her exhibitions have been showcased worldwide. Morris produced the 2016 BBC documentary *My Transgender Summer Camp* and published *You Are You,* a monograph about a camp for gender-expansive children. She lives on Long Island. For more information, visit https://www.lindsaycmorris.com/ or follow at @lindsaymorrisphoto.

Thank you for reading
Rejected: Essays on Belonging

Please leave
a review on your favorite
online bookseller's website

CHECK OUT OTHER GREAT READS FROM
HENRY GRAY PUBLISHING

THE LAST STAGE by Bruce Scivally

Facing his end in his small Los Angeles bungalow, with his Jewish wife, Sadie (Josephine) at his side, famed lawman Wyatt Earp imagines a passing more befitting a man of his reputation: returning to his mining claims in a small desert town, tying up loose ends with Sadie, and – after he strikes gold – confronting a quartet of robbers in a showdown.

VEIL OF SEDUCTION by Emily Dinova

1922. Lorelei Alba, a fiercely independent and ambitious woman, is determined to break into the male-dominated world of investigative journalism by doing the unimaginable – infiltrating Morning Falls Asylum, the gothic hospital to which "troublesome" women are dispatched, never to be seen again. Once there, she meets the darkly handsome and enigmatic Doctor Roman Dreugue, who claims to have found the cure for insanity. But Lorelei's instincts tell her something is terribly wrong, even as her curiosity pulls her deeper into Roman's intimate and isolated world of intrigue.

THE UNDERSTUDY by Charlie Peters

"Tell your boss that I have one of his employees." With those words a kidnapping plot begins in the middle of a high-stakes corporate merger. But the kidnappers' plans don't unfold—they unravel.

"If you're thinking of committing the perfect crime, read Charlie Peters' elegant new thriller first. Find out just how many ways perfection can go wrong." – Dan Hearn, author of *Bad August*

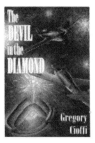

THE DEVIL IN THE DIAMOND by Gregory Cioffi

World War II is coming to a violent close. As the Battle of Okinawa rages on, American soldiers seize Shuri Castle and find a single survivor: Yuujin Miyano. The U.S. private put in charge of watching the prisoner is Eugene Durante. Although enemies, the two men find they have a common multi-generational bond: baseball. Their grandfathers – one in Japan, one in America – bore witness to the magical birth of the game and helped shape it in the 1800s. When the war ends, the two men return to their homes to face a postwar world neither expected. Then both receive messages that change their lives forever: once more, the veterans will face off in a final dramatic clash.

For more info visit HenryGrayPublishing.com

...AND HERE'S MORE PAGE-TURNERS FOR YOUR READING PLEASURE!

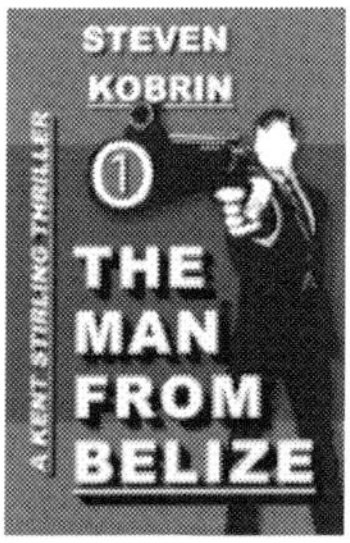
STEVEN
KOBRIN
A KENT STIRLING THRILLER
1
THE
MAN
FROM
BELIZE

THE MAN FROM BELIZE by Steven Kobrin

Life-saving heart surgeon Dr. Kent Stirling lives in paradise, dividing his time between two medical practices in the exotic Yucatan. Deeply in love with the woman of his dreams, he has everything a man could desire... until enemies from his secret past as a government hitman convene to eliminate him, including a death-dealing assassin known as the Viper.

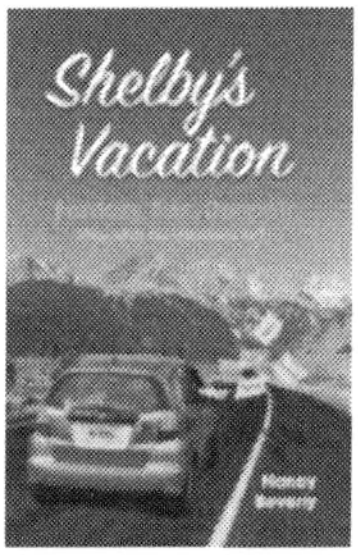
Shelby's
Vacation

SHELBY'S VACATION by Nancy Beverly

Fantasy. Sex. Despair. (Hey, what are vacations for?)

Shelby sets out from L.A. on a much-needed vacation to mend her heart from her latest unrequited crush. By happenstance, she ends up at a rustic mountain resort where she meets the manager, Carol, who has her own memories of the past inhibiting her ability to create a real relationship in the present. Their casual vacation encounter turns into something more profound than either of them bargained for, as each learns what holds them back from living and loving.

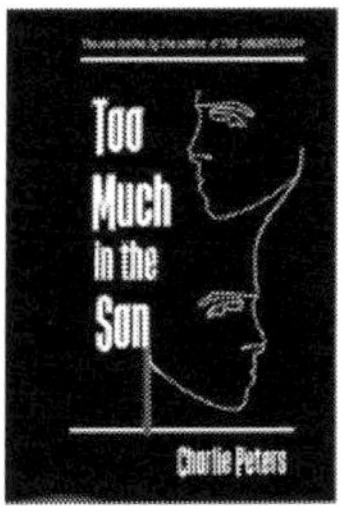
Too
Much
in the
Son
Charlie Peters

TOO MUCH IN THE SON by Charlie Peters

In Martinique, Leo Malone meets Taylor Hoffman, a young man who could be his identical twin. Whey they run afoul of a local gangster, Taylor is murdered and Leo assumes his identity to sneak safely out of the country and back to Los Angeles. But when Taylor's estranged parents meet Leo at the airport, mistaking him for their son, Leo's best-laid plans spiral out of control. Part Agatha Christie, part Elmore Leonard, with a dash of David Mamet and served with a Larry David chaser, *Too Much in the Son* examines the lies, intrigue and violence that make an unexpected family.

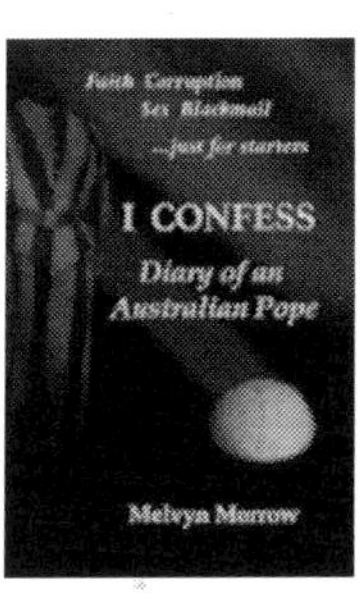
I CONFESS
Diary of an
Australian Pope
Melvyn Morrow

I CONFESS: DIARY OF AN AUSTRALIAN POPE by Melvyn Morrow

"When I became pope, almost the first word the Curia taught me was 'ricatto'—blackmail."

- Pope John XXIV

From acclaimed playwright Melvyn Morrow comes this engrossing tale of an Australian cardinal who has, through extraordinary circumstances, become pope. His personal diary reveals the inner workings of the Vatican and—when he realizes his tenure may be short and begins enacting sweeping reforms—the centuries-old system in place to make sure that the status quo is maintained—at any cost.

For more info visit HenryGrayPublishing.com